Please let us get home

Janet Hickson

Please let us get home

a memoir

D.O.R. Books
Paris

ISBN: 978-0-9568500-0-3
© 2011 Janet Hickson
All rights reserved.
D.O.R. Books, Paris

For Anna and Charlie

Acknowledgements

Rudi Davies for our deep friendship, her unfailing empathy, and positive and helpful criticisms with this book. Debbie Fawcett for managing to put a very untidy manuscript in order.

My father was a cruel man: cruel to his family and cruel to himself. In rain, wasp-stinging sleet and hail, he built a crazy paving terrace outside the drawing-room, dining-room and kitchen French windows, heaving weights of York stone slabs until his hands bled and the crazy paving was blood stained. The summers of my youth, unlike those of my contemporaries, were seasons of black clouds constantly bursting over the garden and frequent thunderstorms crashing murderously over our roof. Summers now seem monotonously calm and unnaturally sunny.

I have heard that when adults revisit the houses in which they lived as children, the houses appear to have shrunk. Cherished memories of imposing mansions dominating acres of garden turn out to be ordinary houses set in manageable little plots. Not long ago, my brother John and I revisited our childhood home. We found that it is a fairly imposing mansion – much, much larger than we thought. The crazy paving is yards wide and stretches the full length of the house – and it has not, over the years, been added to. We remember every bump and ridge and retain, to this day, the scars of wounds they inflicted on our legs and arms as we tripped over them. It is by no means a stately home, but it is undoubtedly a large residence in a good district, with a pretty unmanageable garden, I should say, without my father there to slaughter the weeds, hack down trees and push the mower like an express train up and down the lawns. He did not tend that garden; he ruthlessly, furiously, gloweringly beat it into submission.

My father, Douglas Veale, had pale cold blue eyes, devilish black hair and wickedly thin lips. He plunged, summer and winter, into a cold bath every day before breakfast. On the rare occasions when he succumbed to influenza, he still plunged into the cold bath before going back, outraged by the insubordination of germs, to bed. The houses we lived in were virtually unheated. During the coldest months of the hardest winters, a coal fire would be lit in the drawing-room, but not before teatime. In the mornings, we feeble children dressed and undressed under the bedclothes, but not before a quick dash to the bathroom to splash noisily with one hand, pretending to immerse ourselves in the cold water which he obligingly left for us.

My father was an esteemed Civil Servant, commuting to London every day to climb the ladder of decorations to a knighthood. He would have been a superb commander of a gas chamber in Nazi Germany. He was a superb administrator and the requisite number of Jews to be exterminated daily would have been doubled by him because of streamlined efficiency, his masochistic capacity for hard work, and because, outside the family, he commanded respect, loyalty and unremitting toil from his hand-picked staff; and got it. He also demanded the respect and loyalty of his family but, failing to earn it, didn't command it. John hated him and I was frightened of him. Our loyalty was to each other, not to the tyrannical dictator who ruled and all but ruined our lives.

My mother, Evelyn, was a perfect match for him, and in a distorted way their marriage was one of the most successful, if least happy, I have ever observed. She was a martyr who extracted every ounce of gratification from her martyrdom. She was a peace-lover who stirred up constant wars so that she could inflict peace at any price on the warmongers. Peace at any price except hers. I adored her and she called me her shadow because I never willingly left her side. We fed each other's insatiable neuroses to such an extent that I suffered from chronic nausea.

At the slightest deviation from the narrow path she set me, she would threaten to tell my father. He would then be cross with her and that she couldn't bear – so I must do that, mustn't do the other, must be quiet, good, sad, manageable, ill. She worked permutations of emotional blackmail as a master spy cracks codes. And, when in doubt, there was always the crunch-line, "You'll be sorry when I'm dead." She's been dead for many years now and I am still waiting, without noticeable trepidation, for remorse to engulf me. I did miss her for a moment one summer when I discovered that I had lost her recipe for salad dressing. It was a piquant dressing and a poignant moment. I stood in my kitchen and willed her to dictate it to me. She was, as always, unattainable, and no more difficult to grasp than when she was alive.

She did have redeeming features, though. She was intelligent and witty. She was a heavy smoker and when the cancer scare started, she said, casting a cigarette stub into the pot, " I shall go down with the fags flying." She was elegant, and vain. She had charm. Nevertheless, she had no close friends and I think that was because she had no basic warmth. She was all things to all people. Superficially sympathetic, but without empathy or even sincerity. Is it sincere, if you never forget to ask the grocer how his wife's arthritis is and never forget to tell everyone that you have done so?

Margaret, nicknamed Lally, our elder sister, did one thing for me for which I shall never be able to thank her enough. She taught me to read. At ten years of age, she would race home from school and, literally, teach me everything she had learned that day. Long before I went to school, I had read and read and read. Uncharacteristically, my father let us have the run of his library without censorship. Perhaps the very extent of his un-enlightenment blinded him to the fact that there were passages even in the expurgated edition of *Lady Chatterley's Lover* or *A Passage to India* of which he, himself, would not have approved as suitable reading for a child or a female. I devoured them all between bouts of incapacitating illness. I did not understand all I read. I cherished the words, practicing them in my mind, using them, running a particularly gleaming one for days until another caught my fancy or my father heard one spoken in the wrong context, meaninglessly. My brother noted that it must have been about then that my father wrote me off as being what is now known as educationally sub-normal, although he did, at great financial self-sacrifice I was constantly reminded, send me to school when I was six.

On one occasion, Lally unwittingly caused my first migraine. It happened like this; I was sitting on the swing in the garden when I saw that my mother was sewing on the terrace, and sewing the most beautiful brilliant squares of chiffon in scarlet, cerise, crimson and blue, each square attached to a little black bodice by one corner so that the effect was like a full-blown anemone – of all anemone colours. A flicker of excitement darted through me. It must have been for me and, furthermore, the colours were ravishing. My mother always dressed me in pale pink or green – pink because she said it suited my palest of pale complexions, biliously yellow, I suspect, or green because my grey eyes reflected whatever colour I wore, so that they could seem to be green. Like hers, she said.

In fact, I beat her to it there. My eyes are grey but they are nevertheless greener than hers ever were. Now at last, I thought, I must be going to have something different. I walked over to her and she told me to go back to the swing, she was too busy to talk, the dress had to be finished for Lally to wear at a school play that evening. At that moment, I had my first migraine. What was to become the familiarly-shaped question mark of blinding pain running from one eye to the back of my neck gripped my head in a vice. A few seconds later I was sick. Patiently, my mother mopped up the mess, diagnosed that milk for breakfast did not suit me, put me to lie on the sofa and continued the dressmaking. All that happened on the only sunny morning of my childhood. An anatomy lesson was delayed until the winter.

My parents were out, the maids were in the kitchen and my sister, my brother and I were in the drawing-room. We did not know what to do. Lally, though, thought of an entertainment. She would dance for us, but first she must change into her anemone dress. While she changed, we were to turn out the light. It was winter, after tea, and the flames of the fire would be light enough for the exhibition. The exhibitionism turned out to be uninhibited exhibitionism, and exhibitionism by a sister so 'good,' so reserved that apart from that one spellbinding evening, we can hardly remember her making an impression on us, any difference to our lives at all, except as sole recipient of my father's affection.

She came into the room and started twirling and whirling in the firelight. We were not unduly impressed, but it was better than nothing. Suddenly, she stopped and said, "Shall I take off my knickers?" Without much enthusiasm we agreed that she should. She lifted the petals of her skirt, took off her knickers and then she made an impact that we remember in such vivid detail that we can relive every moment of it. She revealed to us our first sight of pubic hair. Neither of us had had the slightest idea that it existed. She danced again while we crouched lower and lower down on the hearthrug to catch every fascinating glimpse of that thick black, curling crop. Gradually the dancing slowed down and we asked her if everyone got hair on their "you-knows." "Yes," she told us. "Everyone. You're babies, but I expect you will have it too." She squatted between us and showed us more. We saw her clitoris, the damp, red, secret place surrounded by hair as black and curly as that on my father's head. Suddenly, I felt guilty. I KNEW that we were being disgusting. I was not fascinated any more. I was terrified. There was the sound of a key in the latch. My sister, snatching up her knickers, fled from the room and upstairs. We turned on the light. An aura of guilt, shame, horror must have been left in the room. My mother came in looking afraid – or perhaps I projected my fear onto her. But she did not ask what we had been doing. And Lally never danced for us again.

⚜

My attacks of nausea were frequent and at mealtimes, when my father was there, consciously guilt-ridden. Illness was one of the many failings he could not tolerate. A couple of years before my mother died, she succumbed (crept into bed, she called it) to flu. My father glared at her and said:

"How long is this business going to last?"

"I really don't know," quavered my mother, "but I cannot get up today."

With, presumably, a slight feeling of guilt, he called out irritably as he left the house, "Well, is there anything you want? Some jam or something?" Jam. The one thing you want, having weak-mindedly 'crept' to bed with a fever.

My mealtime nausea had to be controlled by me somehow. Apart from other considerations, platefuls of food dizzily wavering in front of me had cost money and, in traditionally nanny-fashion, I was told of the millions of starving children all over the world who would give their right arms, eyes, legs or all three for it. How I wished they would converge on our house, and with what relief I would have sacrificed my share of food. Occasionally, on gazing beseechingly at my mother, she would give me a conspiratorial look, which meant that I could get off my chair and lie down on the floor while the rest of the family ignored the little scene we enacted and munched on at breakneck speed so that my father could, 'Get On.'

However, I devised a fantasy, a safety valve, which often worked. I imagined the inside of my heaving stomach was a sock with a hole in it, and would hold my breath. If I held my breath long enough, a little old lady would come in with a darning mushroom and mend the hole before it burst open and upwards, releasing a gush of vomit onto my plate. Of course, the little old lady would only come if I promised to be good. The origin of the darning lady was from a whimsical child's verse I had learned which described her dressed in grey, and was, metaphorically, a grey cloud appearing over a hill, which might or might not release her beautiful rain. She took a good deal of time off between meals, releasing exceedingly odious rain into basins and bowls, but she and my mother between them, successfully held back the sickness from the dining-room table.

My most reliable bedtime fantasy was the building of a father-proof fortress in which my mother and I could live. That fortress provided endless material with which I could work. It started as a tower built on rock (no quicksand for me), as far inland as possible to go. Access to it had to be arranged for the delivery of medicine, clothes and food, in that order. It was encircled by a moat much too wide for any swimmer, so a drawbridge was added. The drawbridge was a mistake, though. We might forget to pull it up, and it was abandoned in favour of several factories in the tower, thus thwarting any attempts by my father to get at us in our gloomy snuggery, disguised as a chemist or milkman. The factories were entirely automated and produced a limitless quantity of necessities. The tower was built of iron, but metal was a dangerous lightning conductor so even taller towers were build around its vast perimeter, and yet taller towers around them to attract the lightning away from us. We might want to see my brother and sister, so they had a practically equally hazard-proof tower next to ours, with a nanny installed so that my mother's attention would never need to be diverted from me to them. And so it went on. Every imaginable disaster from earthquakes to hurricanes had to be thought of and guarded against. Trusted doctors and nurses had to have cages built for them. Cages to be electrically opened to allow them to emerge in case of illness. Basins, bowls, buckets and lavatories littered every room so that, however sick I was, no floor, furniture or carpet would be soiled. For final, absolute security reasons, I extracted a promise from God that I could depend on. My mother, however old I lived to be, would outlive me. By the time I fell asleep, my tower was impregnable.

I wanted my father to love me. My very first memory of him captures my climbing onto his knee to nestle against his shoulder. To be pushed away, told not to pester him, to 'cut along' to the study and fetch his pipe. I put flowers in my hair on Sundays when he came sternly, self-righteously home to breakfast from Holy Communion. He was angry with my mother, she told me, because I was vain and silly. The double guilt of vanity and making him cross with her stopped the titivating. I burnished up my intelligence instead. One Sunday morning, I had announced to a stunned family audience that Mrs Broadbent, the headmistress of St. Helen's School, Northwood, had asked for me to be sent up to the 'big school' to read aloud to her. It was true that my fluent reading astonished the head of the kindergarten because, of course, my sister had turned me into an apparent infant prodigy. The rest was a totally uncalculated, unexpected lie and I was as stunned as the rest of them. My father's attention was caught at last. He half smiled at me and I was nearly happy. If only it could have been left at that, but Monday inexorably follows Sunday, and on Monday an inquisition was enacted about my spectacular sortie into the 'big school.' Who had taken me? The school was the other side of a main road and the 'little ones' were not allowed into it except for dancing classes to which they were taken by their mothers. What did I read? What did the headmistress say? How long was I there? Did I go to her study? Had I seen any of my sister's friends? Out came the lies and they were so plausible, so convincing, and so perilously easy that I almost believe now in the unique distinction of having, at the age of six, read aloud in response to an unprecedented request to the fascinated headmistress of a large school. I jumped all the hurdles faultlessly and thought the incident had been forgotten. My father grudgingly dished out a tiny ration of modest praise. Did he suspect? Did he feel threatened by a possible ability to lie, which might stem from an intelligence sharper than his? He was clever, but not flexible enough to acknowledge that he could ever be wrong. Now, when my brother and I argue, the loser, at the moment of defeat or boredom, will quote the old man's clinching punch line, a phrase which punctuated our lives like a proliferation of full-stops. "Well, whatever you say or think, I can assure you I am right."

Wednesday arrived and my mother took me to the 'big school' for dancing class. The headmistress sat beside her. I thought I had forgotten the reading-aloud adventure. Not so. Panic swamped me and I felt a hot trickle bursting through my pants, running down my legs to splash past socks, bronze dancing pumps, and spread into a puddle on the floor at my feet. My mother leapt into her star-role. She gathered me up, apologising to the headmistress, apologising to the dancing mistress, Mrs Grant, apologising to the other mothers, and I was hustled home amidst a confusing blend of solicitude at my humiliating 'accident' and bewilderment that the headmistress, by detonating my reading-aloud time bomb, had discovered me "telling a story." My father would have to know. I wasn't sure whether he was to hear about the lie, which seemed very trivial, or the 'accident,' of which I was deeply ashamed. At home she put me to bed. She supposed I must have a chill. I could snuggle down and she would look after me.

Anyway, back to the lie, or was it the dancing class? There must have been a deadly dearth of drama during the last few days or surely such a militant pacifist would have let the matter drop. But no! War had to be waged. She was overflowing with oil to pour on troubled waters.

Directly my father came home from administering his ministry, I heard her tearful whining floating up from the hall. My father hectored, raged and finally stampeded upstairs. Self-pity is a very underrated emotion and if now I were unable to weep for the little girl I was then, I think I would be a cooler friend, a woman with less time for the sad people who cross her path. But I can cry as I cried then. My father sat on the end of the bed and lacerated me with words. "If you were a boy," he said, "I should beat you to within an inch of your life." He was a believer in capital punishment for most of the criminal population, and flogging for the rest. I had sinned. I had sinned. I had sinned. That was the main theme. I see myself, sitting bolt upright, tears streaming from huge greenish-grey eyes, which in photographs look too heavy for the tiny, white face in which they were set. Speechless. There was no explanation. Apologies were scorned. Vows never to lie again were not to be trusted – how could they be when I was already a self-condemned serial liar? Most terrifying of all, any sin, any deviation, however slight, would not be tolerated in his house. The sinner would be turned out – homeless. His parting shot was, "May God forgive you; I NEVER can." My mother eventually came to tuck me up and kiss me goodnight. Her kiss was as light, and as dry, as a moth fluttering for a moment against my cheek. I always begged for a 'wet' kiss. I needed a healthy, hearty, jolly hug. I kick myself now for not having dressed, walked out of the house and presented myself at the police station with the sensational news that my father, a respected civil servant, a likeable neighbour, a weekly – overt at any rate – Christian and regular communicant, had just evicted me for telling a lie. "Could I," I ought to have asked, "be directed to the nearest Dr. Barnardo's Home?"

Sophisticated behaviour for a six-year-old, but a delicious fantasy.

But not lying in moments of panic is very hard to avoid as a small child. Quite soon after the reading aloud episode, I was caught again. It was Easter and I had been given a chocolate shaped like a fish and wrapped in gold paper. It was so beautiful that, while the others were guzzling their chocolate eggs, I preserved my fish in spite of pleas to unwrap it and taste it. I decided to keep it forever. Evening came and I put the fish on the chair beside the bed, while being undressed and bathed. As I nestled down into bed, I stroked my fish and a slither of gold paper came away and I licked the chocolate on my fingers again and again until I had eaten a whole fin. My father passed the door, saw my chocolate stained face and asked whether I had been eating the fish. I absolutely denied that I had. He hoped I would be sick as punishment for my lie.

God may have been too busy making numerous other children sick as a punishment for Easter greed to bother about a really hardened sinner like me. Very soon after that though, one of my numerous diets banned chocolate. I am sure chocolate is nourishing and that were I ever to find myself on a desert island with no record player, no music and no books, but an island simply littered with chocolate fish, it would be a matter of minutes before I discarded my loathing of it. As things are, I just cannot be bothered, and remain happily anti-chocolate while those around me chew, gobble, enjoy and digest the revolting stuff.

Of course, as I grew up, I learnt to lie and learnt all the inherent dangers of lying too. I had to remember which lie I had told to which person, and to which person I had confessed to having lied to someone else. My guilt made it imperative to confess every lie to someone. I almost never resort to anything but the whitest of white lies now, because by the time I was grown up the necessity to lie to my parents, out of sheer self-preservation, had become such a habit that even when I was telling the naked, unadorned, un-enhanced truth, I was beset by an uncomfortable feeling that I was lying.

John, my brother and friend, the adversary whom I fought during infrequent, guilty attacks of good health, but who was comfortingly unconquerable, my confidant and companion was – at birth – large, strong and, according to my mother, arrogant. It is difficult to envisage an hour-old arrogant infant but, as she frequently told us, my mother's worst enemy could not accuse her of dishonesty or of being a possessive mother and, above all, she maintained, she was a *good judge of character* and, as far as my brother was concerned, I think she was. He was certainly resilient and incredibly obstinate.

Unconquerable, I said. But once, having run through *Pig, Swine, Baby* and the usual derisive terms children use, I searched wildly for a really appalling insult. "You smell of brown sugar," I shouted. No reaction. "Stuffed Wireless," I heard myself shriek. To my consternation, he burst into tears. At last I had, unwittingly, found a chink in his armour. I still don't know why it had that disquieting effect. Unhappily, he grew defences, and if I felt like hurting him, I was lost. Further than "Stuffed Wireless" I seem unable to go! And his arrogance kept company with him into adulthood, though by then, perhaps, it was integrity.

To the outside world we must have appeared to be a typical, conventionally united, happy family. When on view to the public my father acted with admirable finesse the role of devoted husband and father, and one of the scenes in the play was *The English Family Plays Cricket in The Garden*. There was a certain amount of dissembling here. My father, and therefore my sister, actually enjoyed cricket, in mackintoshes and Wellington boots in the rain-soggy garden. My mother, ever anxious to sacrifice herself for peace, pretended, making sure the pretence was noted, to enjoy it. I hated it, loathed running and being hit on the shins. Moreover, I dreaded my father shouting "butter-fingers" at me when my fielding fell short of Test Match standard. My brother John simply refused to play unless he was allowed to bat all the time. He refused, at the age of four, not knowing that if he didn't snatch the opportunity of winning the as yet unforeseen Second World War on the battlefield of our garden, he would be flogged for disobedience. And flogged he was, to the accompaniment of the wails of my mother and myself, over and over again, and still he refused. However, it limbered him up for Repton, where he didn't refuse to play unless he batted all the time. He refused because he found it more important to compose a clarinet concerto, parts of which were later to be included in a more mature work performed at a Promenade Concert in the Albert Hall.

His arrogance had to be seen to be believed. It blossomed un-blighted by my mother's hold on him. In fact, she was so absorbed in cultivating my frailty, that she relieved herself of all responsibility for John by handing him over to a wholesome nanny who adored him, and whose adoration he reciprocated. I, of course, lived up to expectations by screaming every time the nanny came near me, even refusing to let her darn my socks because she licked the cotton before threading the needle, a chore my mother outwardly sadly but exultantly undertook to the deafening applause of the angels who await the arrival in heaven of long-suffering mothers.

My father, perhaps also noting John's arrogant birthday expression, instantly decided that he was destined for the army. The very strictest discipline was necessary to be remembered and emulated when leading the regiments he would one day command. For a boy, discipline involved regular flogging on the slightest pretext. Moreover, flogging, to be effective, must be dreaded for hours, preferably days, in advance, so apart from spur-of-the-moment punishment, Friday nights were flogging nights. However, carefully drawn-up campaigns go wrong. My brother did not take his punishment like a man. He did not keep a stiff upper lip. He didn't even whimper like a coward; cowards are not such a dead loss. They often mature into respectable bullies. He was, psychologically, unbeatable. He fought back, kicking, screaming, furious. John was arrogant and angry. Tin soldiers bored him. Toy guns gathered dust. He needed arguments, reasons, music. He did not accept my father as an authoritarian figure to be obeyed.

My mother and I pleaded with him to give way for the sake of peace, of course. But John wouldn't pay the price of losing his own integrity and fought on. Gradually all rules became challenges, all pronouncements questioned, and in a different social setting he would almost certainly have become a delinquent.

At astronomical financial sacrifice for which he remained stubbornly ungrateful, he was sent to Repton. He and I shared an inability to feel and express instant gratitude, on demand. He was openly resentful and I once, in a moment of great daring, said I would have been thankful never to have been born. My father believed that the Officers' Training Corps at a 'good public school' would, at last, open my brother's eyes to the joys of commanding subordinates. Actually, the "Stuffed Wireless" refused even to become a prefect, thus evading the dubious delights of caning little new boys, fags half his size.

The boys slept in different houses, but met in classrooms for lessons. They were not allowed to visit each other in their different houses after dusk. Who knows what unspeakable vices might flourish in the dark? My brother would, presumably, have been safe because my father had warned him before he went to Repton that even in the Best Public School, he might find the odd "Joy-boy." Nevertheless a boy who preferred 'sissy' symphonies to cricket would be particularly suspect and expelled forthwith as a dangerous pervert if found in the wrong house. But one night he tossed and turned for ten agonising minutes trying to remember the name of the boy who sat next to him in Geography lessons but was in a different house. He went through all the permutations of the alphabet without success. By ZA? ZB? ZC? the strain was unbearable. He marched fearlessly out of his own house and broke through a window into the house which he hoped the nameless boy inhabited. He searched the dormitories, found his quarry, woke him up, asked him his name and, with a blissful sigh of relief, strolled, muttering "Watson. Watson," and doubtless, "Sherlock Holmes" as an aide memoire, back to bed, past the oblivious prefects and fell placidly to sleep.

Towards the end of the war, my father's ambitions for him were partially realised. But the pill was bitter. My conscripted brother refused a commission, evaded having a decent crack at Jerry and, by a process of intimidating successive commanding officers, gradually slithered, without a single medal, from the distinguished Rifle Brigade into the ignominious ranks of the non-combatant Army Education Corps. What relief each of his commanding officers must have received, when notice was given that the sharpest thorn in their flesh was to be posted elsewhere. It was perfectly simple. My brother, whenever charged with an offence, questioned the validity of *King's Regulations*.

"I take it, then, Sir, that my Army Pay book is correct?"

Irritation. "Of course your Army Pay book is O.K."

"In that case, Sir, must I accept the fact that my hair is blue and my eyes brown?"

His last gesture as a soldier was to close the office of the Education Corps, at which he alone was stationed, by throwing away all the files and settling down to compose music in peace. But not without one disquieting incident. One of his duties had been to visit military hospitals to supervise the welfare of the enlisted men. At a hospital in Wiltshire, the matron asked him for felt for four men to make soft toys in Occupational Therapy. Ever eager to help the gallant lads back to the war as fast as possible – but without him – John hastened to send off Army Order Form XZY for felt. Being neither practical nor conscientious, he invented what he assumed would be about the correct amount. Six truck loads of purple felt had to be shunted into a siding at a railway station in Wiltshire and are, in all probability, still there.

※

The sexes in our house were rigidly segregated – up to a point. My parents' bedroom door, usually kept shut anyway, was twice slammed in my face – once when I caught a glimpse of my father in vest and pants, and once when I caught a back view of my brother, young enough to have a thermometer inserted by my mother into his chubby bottom. When my mother was at home, she bathed me, and while she was tucking me into bed, John was bathed and bedded by a nursemaid.

When my mother was out, the cook, Phyllis, took over bathing me. I loved her – she was not the threatening baby-minder my brother's nanny was – and I was her favourite of the three children. She had a vast plaited bun of red hair which I coveted and sometimes she would unpin it and drape it over my head for me to feel how it would be if I were ever allowed to grow my hair. At times I would attach an old Shetland shawl to my head and try to brush and comb it.

Phyllis had a "follower," a plumber, who, at her command, used to attempt inexpertly to let off fireworks in the garden on Guy Fawkes nights. Between Catherine wheels stubbornly refusing to rotate, squibs diving, spluttering into the ground, and fantastically beautiful sparklers, one for each of us, there was always a rocket which seemed to be magnetically drawn to Phyllis's red hair, which was inflammable and yet, it seemed, constructed of asbestos. I remember her, head in flames, hastily smothered in the plumber's overcoat – but no lasting damage was done.

After a very long "walking out" period, the announcement of a forthcoming engagement and an eternity of formal betrothal, she married the plumber in spite, or because of his undeviating skill of aiming missiles at her. John's nursemaid also left to be replaced by a quiet, dim, country girl, Hilda, to whom he fickly and immediately transferred his love.

The new nursemaid, when in charge of both of us at bedtime, bathed us together. I asked the girl why it was that I had not got a tail in front like John. Confused, she said she would have to ask my mother. I was confused too and searched and searched for my penis. Instinct must have prevented me asking my mother myself, but enlightenment was at hand. New nanny, Hilda, became friendly with another nanny down the road who had been installed in readiness for the birth of a baby. John and I were taken to see the new baby and I shuddered with horror at the thought of the rough passage he had had being born.

He was smothered in bandages – or, to be precise, two bandages. One covered his "tummy-button" (rude expression, not to be used in public) and the other was wrapped round his poor little "tail." The bandages were removed while we watched him being bathed, and we were terribly shocked. The bandages had tiny bloodstains, were thrown away, renewed, and all to a chorus of nanny-talk about afternoons off, letters from home and the milkman. Afterwards, my brother was more callous than I was. He could afford to be. He miraculously, had survived his infancy intact. I, it appeared, must have suffered even more acutely than the baby down the road. With me, they had gone too far, and cut it right off. My brother told me that that was what they did to make girls.

For weeks I intermittently screamed with envy and rage at my brother. My mother was astounded. Her little girl could not hate her own brother. And from our nursery departed a beautiful, dapple-grey rocking horse. For some seemingly obscure reason, I had taken to screaming with fright at its flaring red nostrils as well.

As the screaming slowly diminished, I became resigned to my brother's superiority. I needed him again and, most of the time, forgot my wounds. We asked if we could have our rocking horse back and were taken up to the attic to see it, its head swathed in sacking bandages. I wanted the bandages removed. I promised not to scream. I remembered its head and nostrils and I assured my mother that I would not be frightened, but my mother thought it wiser, safer, to leave him where he was. We never saw him again.

I consciously resented John's vigour and size that led to the injustice of his spreading over to my side of the twin pram we shared. However, we stuck to the rules. He liked outings but insisted on his full quota of being pushed in the pram, I preferred riding in the pram, but legs aching, uncomplainingly slogged my turns of walking. Envy was part of the dark side of my personality which had to be repressed because my mother's favourite child had been born in her image with all the human virtues and none of its vices. Even Lally scored a point with her there. She had never, my mother vowed, been the slightest bit jealous of John and me. On the contrary, she had had to be restrained from smothering us to death by heaping all her toys on us when we disrupted the threesome of my parents and herself, thus appearing to live up to my mother's ideal of ever-loving, never-hating brothers and sisters.

I had horrifying nightmares of bashing my brother's head on the terrace until he was dead and burying him in the garden.

I was horrified at the memory of these nightmares of murder and the horror was mostly attached to the murder itself, but added to it was terror of the rage my father would unleash at the disorganisation it would make in the serried ranks of flowers which leapt to attention in the garden on his instructions.

For the whole of August, the ministry had to struggle along without my father's administrative zeal. Like well-trained dogs, I expect they obeyed the rules without noticing that the "Master" was away. It was hell for us, though. Parents, daughters, son and two maids embarked for the Nautical Drill of the Annual Holiday. A furnished house was rented in cold, damp Cornwall. We saw very little of the house because arrangements had been made the previous year for the hire of a small rowing boat and, from the minute we unpacked our mackintoshes until the moment they had become too leaky to repack for the homeward journey and were buried at sea, we rowed, were rowed, and rowed again from Looe to Fowey, from Fowey to Looe and from Looe towards the horizon, occasionally trespassing, in passing, for ten minutes on Looe Island for the daily enforced bathe or the necessary squatting behind rocks. The maids had a working holiday carrying out the ordinary routine of home life among the inconveniences of cheap, porridge-coloured rented houses. We seldom disembarked. Lunch and tea breaks were cut to the minimum. The anchor was tossed overboard, often pointlessly, as we were too far into mid-ocean for it to reach the seabed. We crouched over wet sandwiches and saffron cake, the boat plunging and rising, and before we knew where we were – not that it made any difference, with no land in sight – it was time to weigh anchor and *Get On*. My father sat in the middle of the boat, rowing as though his life depended on it. Indeed, only too often all our lives did depend on it. And when blood spurted from his blisters he would lean happily on the oars for a minute and say, "Now the holiday is doing me good." Lally curled up on the anchor rope in the bow of the boat, my mother, in a faded Burberry and old felt hat decorated with seagull droppings, wielded the tiller at the stern, and John and I perched on the thwarts port and starboard of her. I know rowing boat phraseology. We had to use it.

I was so frightened of the sea, I used to bury my head in her lap and pray, "Please God, make Daddy take us home. Please God, let us get back and I'll NEVER be naughty again. Please let us get home." But praying itself was naughty because it put the boat out of trim. "Sit up, you there, and shift to starboard. No, too far. Shift half an inch to port again. Look lively," the commands would be shouted. I was so frightened, and knew it, that I didn't have to feel sick. I was a marvellous sailor.

Nothing deterred my father. According to him, the sea was always "as calm as a duck pond" (choppy), "a bit choppy today but nothing to worry about" (rough), "choppy" (dangerous), or a "bit rough" (stormy enough for an incompetent harbour master to forbid risking the lives of seamen crewing fishing boats for a living). So rough, in fact, that the waves fought each other as well as us. Sometimes there was a "pleasant" ground swell – enormous waves so gigantic that, juddering in the troughs between them, mountainous seas fore and aft seemed almost to meet overhead.

Once, when the harbour master confined the Looe fishing fleet of trawlers to harbour because of tempestuous seas, he couldn't control our skipper and across the bar we plunged and lurched. My brother and I hated rowing but we had to. We had to learn how to row and feather the oars because everyone has to learn how to row a boat, and we had to row to escape the unbelievable discomfort of sitting hour after hour, dead-still, on those damnable narrow thwarts flanking my mother.

Within seconds of my orders to "take an oar there," I was longing for release. Dragging an oar through choppy seas at the age of, say, nine, is backbreaking, and the others were all so much stronger than I was that my mother had to push frantically at the tiller to stop the boat whizzing round in circles. Another hazard was that if I rowed from the thwart behind my father, I had to keep time with his cutting, lashing of the waves and, if I sat in front of him and limply let up momentarily on my tickling of the sea's surface, his oar would jab me painfully in the back. Rhythm in rowing is essential. Also, when my wrists gave way and, nautically speaking, I caught a crab, the end of the oar I was holding leapt up under my chin with such force it ought to have broken my neck.

Those holidays were the times I came nearest to seeing the family as it really was. I vowed that when I was grown-up, I would never bathe again. I would never let my children go in a boat or swim. I would never, never, go to the seaside at all. The worst days were Saturdays because, as Friday nights were flogging nights for John, so were Friday nights Syrup of Figs night for me, and my father could not, must not, know that bodily functions functioned. I would hold on as long as I could, but in the end I would have to be held ignominiously over the side of the heaving boat, thus putting it yet again out of trim, while my father made angry clicking noises at the back of his nose; something between a disgusted snort and a contemptuous grunt. We were taught to ship the oars, unship the oars, ordered to clutch at slimy rocks with the boathook, but we never learnt how to leap from the boat onto the beach or jetty, according to the time of day and state of the tide, without bruising our shins.

People sometimes ask if I have been to Cornwall. I usually say that I have not because the only bits of it I might know are hidden under crashing grey waves ridden by crazy white horses. The waves broke over the bows of the boat and we had to look sharp, lift the floorboard and bale out with empty pilchard tins, the sharp edges fraying our fingers.

Once my father took us out on a very stormy day with only one pair of oars in the boat. One oar broke and somehow he got us back to the harbour, skirting jagged reefs of rocks in a hideously angry sea, by waggling the remaining oar out of the stern from which the rudder, the tiller and my mother had been removed. He did do it. But if he hadn't, and I think most people couldn't, it would have been suicide and murder. I can understand the appeal the sea had for him. There they were, two furious, destructive, cruel forces fighting each other. And there we were, my mother, my brother and myself, huddled cold and clammy in the stern of the boat, detesting every second of it. At least John and I did. It suited my mother to shiver, showing us occasional ineffectual light pats on our sea-wet hands that she "understood" and was protective of her children, while bored, submissive, aloofly enduring, in the centre of the battle. I shall never forgive them for those month-long summer holidays in Cornwall holidays during which the comforting phrases were "only two more Wednesdays now," "only one more Sunday," and finally, "this time tomorrow, we shall be home, touch wood." The worm ought to have turned and refused to allow children to be exposed to such danger. The admiral *manqué* ought to have waited until his crew were old enough to mutiny. It was not funny, though we have dined out on those incredible seaside family holidays for years. The thought has just struck me. We didn't have buckets and spades. There would have been no time to use them.

Those were the early days of my childhood: rain, nausea, vomit, fright, and fantasies. Prayers that I would die before my mother, prayers that she would live forever, that my father wouldn't be angry with the her-me person, and prayers that enough books would be written to last me all my life. Now my fear is that I shall die before I've read the mountains of words waiting for me. In books I recognise a lifeline, which I thought could not be broken.

The most fervent of all my prayers was that I would be good, would not lose control, be submerged in black melancholy, scream, kill or go mad. Later, of course, my lifeline of books did snap because I broke down, could not concentrate, was shattered, hysterical, nearly screamed and had to go into "one of those places," as my mother called psychiatric hospitals, to regress and be cared for, healed and, as an out-patient, gradually learn from doctors how to be furious and free, how to hate, love and be loved.

When my father was seconded from the Ministry of Health to Oxford, where he was Registrar of the University, we left our childhood home in Ducks Hill Road, Northwood, Middlesex and moved to an enormous Victorian edifice in North Oxford. The house was on the corner of Church Walk and Winchester Road and opposite North Parade with its little row of shops. Among the shops was a chemist. I was nine years old when we moved and weighed exactly three stone. I was sent there every Friday after lunch to stand on the scales and every week if I had gained an ounce or two, I was rewarded with a penny or two.

My mother's diagnosis of my problem with nausea (she had trained as a nurse) was called Acidosis and when I succumbed to these episodes it was said to be 'Janet having an attack'. The attacks were the result of whatever I had eaten for the last meal. "It must have been the banana," and the next day when offered a banana I would refuse it as it made me ill the previous day.

"Oh, but darling, this wouldn't make a fly sick," my mother would say, "Oh well, what about this?" holding out a grape. In the end, after years of this, a solution was found. My mother decided that my diet should be almost exclusively Brand's Chicken Essence, barley sugar in the form of twisted sticks and Vichy water. I must have had some other sources of nourishment to survive until I was sixteen and had a period, grew taller and better, until menstruation started again a year later.

I am as I am because and in spite of what happened to me. The neuroses are contained. The habit of illness has been broken. I have acquired not instant resilience, but, given time to percolate, it rears up when necessary and my spirit is unbroken.

When I was sixteen, I experimented with colourless nail varnish. My father noticed, or did my mother sadly stir up trouble by reporting it? He was repelled. I was not allowed to pass anything to him at mealtimes – in fact, I was forbidden to touch anything he might touch. However, I continued to use my nail varnish, disregarding with considerable trepidation his threats of eviction. He said I was disobedient and he would break my spirit. I thought to myself: "You make me suffer. I may go mad. But you will NEVER break my spirit." Brave thoughts because, it so happened, eviction was in the air. John went up to Oxford and grew, with incautious abandon, a beautiful, bushy, russet-coloured beard, thus anticipating those charming, considerate, idealistic young men who look like kind gorillas – and even their fuddy-duddy fathers who sprout side-whiskers almost to their chins. By that time, John was too tall to flog, and suffering from vertigo badly enough to make him giddy on top of a stepladder, he preferred not to stand up at all in case of an attack. He was refused admittance to the house. He fell into the arms and bed of a girl who wanted him. Several girls and several abortions later, he married one of them, Diana Taylor, an artist who worked at The Playhouse in Beaumont Street. When, eventually, my mother had devised a precarious peace between my father and brother, John came to call. My father's attention had to be drawn to a fact he had not noticed – John was, of his own free will, once more clean-shaven.

John was in favour again, and I was still frustrated by not reaching my potential. But Oh! The dancing. My mother was obsessed by, dependent on and loved and hated my delicacy. Stupidity is easily forgiven, understood, ignored and forgotten, but intelligence neglected when it is so vitally needed, so essential for survival and could turn a downward spiral into a spiralling rocket, leaves a lasting bitterness. All the diets concocted for me, the rests in bed, the battles within myself not to let her down by getting better, could have been hurled like confetti in all directions if only I had been allowed to dance. I was born to be a ballet dancer. My big toes and the two next to them are of equal length. My bones turn naturally outward. In one way, I was fortunate. At both my schools, St. Helen's in Northwood, and Wychwood in Oxford, the dancing mistresses were not officially on the school staff. They visited from London. School rules meant nothing to them, and heaven must open its gates to them for their stubborn, categorical refusal to keep me in the right classes for my age. I was, against the advice and wisdom of headmistresses, promoted outright into the top classes, in front of the front row of girls, there to demonstrate the steps, the artistry, to head-girls, prefects, seniors, mothers, visitors, the lot. And on dancing class days, I was never sick. Two and two did not, however, make four. When I changed schools, dancing classes ceased in the summer and gave way, for some obscure reason, to rounders! One summer I had school phobia right up to the last two weeks of term, and I clung to my mother like a leech and was sicker than ever.

For terms and terms beforehand, I had always, when bicycling to school, had desperate forebodings. Not that school would be worse than usual but that by the time it was over, I would find that, without me there, our house would have burnt to the ground, war would have broken out, or unimaginable catastrophes would have occurred and my mother would have gone. Not only my mother, but the rest of them, including the house, would have disappeared and I should go home to – nothing. No mother, no brother, no father, not even a house. I would be a lost, helpless, nothingness, apart from the tiny bit of me that would know that they had vanished and that I was non-existent.

That summer term, I would not, could not go to school. Even my mother was more anxious than usual, more than anxious – alarmed. For her own emotional security, reasons, however implausible, had to be found, and such a prolonged illness could not be attributed to food, and "just your nerves" for a whole term was a bit too un-nerving. She did not approach the school to find out, face and discuss difficulties that might have arisen there. She had a subtler plan. She would, she said, take me herself one afternoon to watch the girls playing rounders and she would stay with me all the time. She wrote to the headmistress to say that I had been ill but was now convalescent, and off to school we rode on our bicycles.

When we arrived I felt better. I left my mother and went to play with some other girls. At the end of the afternoon I looked round and my mother had vanished. The disaster that had been looming over me for so long had arrived. The other girls collected hats, shoes and bicycles and, laughing and talking in little groups, went home. I was stranded, mouth dry with fear, drowning in waves of nausea, shaking with terror. I collected my bicycle from the stand next to the now sickeningly empty one where my mother had propped hers, and set off for the rubble, the ghost of what had once been home. I remember a strange woman stopping me to ask if I were all right – she was so insistent that I had to dismount to say politely, as I had been brought up to do: "Yes, thank you."

"Are you sure?" she persisted.

"Yes, thank you." Urgently.

I wobbled off and, when I got there, the house was still erect. I threw down my bicycle and staggered into the hall, shouting,

"Mummy, Mummy!"

"Yes, darling?"

"Where were you?"

"I saw you playing and just slipped away so that you wouldn't notice."

Her plan failed and I continued to cling. However, two weeks before the end of term, my brother, in intense pain, unknowingly helped me back to school. He had to have a mastoid operation. Doctors and specialists were called, conferred gloomily, and my brother was whisked to a nursing home, where for days he lay dangerously ill.

In a muddled, dismal way, I felt that, while he was so ill, my mother and the house would be safe and back to school I went. In some ways it was better than school phobia, but I was so distraught about John, and knew the reality of what was frightening me so much that, once again, I didn't have to feel sick.

My mother was delighted that her ingenious plan for getting me back to school had worked. John recovered and she settled down happily to less drawn-out disasters. Her yes-girl was just better enough to suit her but was still, thank goodness, not well enough to say: "No, I've been on the inside looking out for too long, and now I propose to join the outside world."

No one twigged that if rounders had given way to dancing, I would have made miraculous recoveries, at least on those days. But in any case, the dancing was not ballet. Central European, Greek, Ballroom, you name it, I excelled at it. I begged, pleaded, and swore eternal goodness, from the age of seven onwards, to have ballet lessons. The very idea of such extravagant, useless additional expenditure reduced my father to puce-faced rage. Lally was at boarding school, how could he afford ballet lessons when we were, he implied, already living in the shadow of the workhouse because of the financial sacrifices he was continually, ostentatiously and, apparently, most unwillingly making to keep us alive. I nagged. He refused. Friends bearded him in his office to tell him a star was not being born. A Russian impresario offered to take me to Russia to train for the Russian Ballet. My father was furious at the intrusion, the waste of time, and the impertinence of that intrepid Russian. Finally, he played his trump card. I could never, anyway, appear on a stage, he said, because I had a hump.

My father's best friend was Sir Eric Bamford, Chairman of the Board of Inland Revenue, and as an honorary uncle, he was my favourite visitor to our house. He was raked in for advice on my ballet ambitions and was alleged to have pronounced on its total unsuitability for me.

Lally's diagnosis, when years later as a student at Bedford Physical Training College she was qualified to voice her professional opinion, was that as I suffered from winged scapulae, any career involving stage appearances would be unthinkable. Literally, physically unable to face the reality, I examined my reflection, three-quarter backwards, in a long looking glass with a hand mirror. One shoulder blade protruded. I was convinced. And so complete was the conviction that when I emerged into undergraduate society and embarked on a dazzling, hectic round of parties, I always had my dresses made with boleros or cut high at the back.

That back which is as straight as a board and strong as steel.

If a piano has to be moved or a car pushed, I am the one to do it, but invite me to the ballet and I cannot go. My mental hump, the heaviest chip on my shoulder, plagues me like a slipped disc at the sight of ballerinas dancing, exquisitely, yes, but roles which I could have danced, stolen from me by my father's blindness, meanness and finally blatant trickery.

When I was seventeen, at least thirteen years too late, with sadistic irony he suddenly, uselessly gave way, and I was sent to a ballet class. I was not the only one to weep at the frustration of wasted talent. Miss Betts was a good teacher but it was so much too late that the lost years could never be recovered. She told me what I already knew. She wept for me too, because she knew what I had missed, that if only, *if only* I had been trained, I would have been a great dancer. As it was, I could never catch up with the technique.

During all those years, since I was four and saw an elderly ballet dancer heaving herself onto her points to execute a tired pirouette in a pantomime, I knew that dancing was my life. I never visualised my name in lights at Sadler's Wells. I never imagined tidal waves of applause. I never thought of an audience, footlights, myself the ballerina, spotlight, fame or fortune. All I wanted was great music to which I could dance. And, for me, dancing was freedom. An opera was performed and produced in Oxford by professionals, the chorus alone enlisted from the amateur ranks of the University Opera Society. I don't remember how I got in on the act but I did and I was persuaded to do the choreography.

It was as easy as beating a blind man at tiddlywinks, but it attracted good notices and, to my amazement, I was called on stage to take a solo curtain call as the dance arranger. Karl Rankl conducted the opera, saw me in the chorus, noticed my name in the programme and, acting on his own initiative, joined the long line of failed advocates on my behalf by telling my father that I ought to be, must be trained as a choreographer. His impudence was quietly and effectively snubbed.

The rigid discipline of training, married to the ethereal grace and unreality of the ballet might have repressed the raging conflict seething within me, resolving itself into a harmonious blend of my authoritarian father and unattainable, Holy Grail-type mother. From an emotionally deprived environment the rigorous but cherished life of a ballerina might have kept depression in the wings.

⁂

School holidays, after John left the Dragon School in Oxford and went to Repton to learn "How to Keep the Empire in Its Place", were dangerous for my mother, my brother and myself. The hazard for my mother was that John and I were too close for safety. We were perilously close. We amused each other and played together.

I was never ill when he was there and my feeling well was a threat to her hold over me. It meant that I left her side to be with him and played with fire in doing so. Her love for me faltered as she helplessly watched us enjoying each other's company. He led me into taking emotional risks – the worst of which was daring occasionally to disagree with her.

The slightest disagreement upset her, made her feel ill, made me feel guilty and sharply brought me into line again. She was not afraid of my being mashed by a car during my rare visits to and from school, but John and I went for bicycle rides together and what's more bicycling was so "unfeminine." She bicycled herself and was not a transvestite but he and I together – that was a different thing. She was a very long way from being above attempts to manipulate fights between John and me. She took him aside and told him, in confidence, that she had a weak heart and had been warned that worry was bad for it. She took me aside and told me, confidentially, that she had told my brother she had a weak heart because he was so exhausting she hoped to frighten him into meeker behaviour, but in case he told me what she had said I was not to worry. She had not even been to a doctor, she said, and was perfectly well. My brother told me his side of the story and I told mine.

Her ploy paid off for her. I assumed that what she had told me was a white lie. She knew that I would be paralysed with terror if I gave it in such a way that I was convinced that she was dissembling. She was ill. I raged at John both for tiring her and for disbelieving her. Our friendship suffered a temporary setback and I became meekly ill myself again. Her heart thumped away soundly until she died at the age of 84.

The danger of school holidays for John was of a different order altogether. Among others there were two overtly sinister homosexuals on the list of my father's friends. One was the distinguished don, Neville Coghill. He did not, unfortunately, confine his activities to taking a fancy to one or two students, treating them to theatres and concerts and projecting a harmless patron-like figure of himself. His taste lay more in the direction of sexual intimacy.

The other one was not a don at all – he was a Catholic priest, Lyttleton Powys, who lived with and cosseted a moth-eaten-looking old mother. The priest was perpetually swaddling the old mother in more and more shawls of varying shades of grey in his efforts to protect her from draughts. She was like a cocoon with her wizened grey face peering out from the layers of grey shawls. Their house was opposite ours.

My father must have known about their afflictions – if afflictions they can be called. With the population explosion and the Wolfenden Report it would seem that the more homosexuals are encouraged, helped and urged to gratify their desires, the happier and safer everyone will be and I can think of no more innocuous way of life.

However, my father, like a distinguished War Lord, went

into inarticulate paroxysms of rage at the mention of *That Vice*. He had warned John of the possibility of finding 'Joy-Boys', as he called them, at Repton, but he gratefully accepted, on my brother's behalf, invitations from those two men to go to stay with them at their little country cottages during school holidays. John hated the don – not on account of his unwelcome advances but because of his dislikeable personality. He liked the priest – they went riding together and he was, in any case, a nice, kind, good man. John was willing to repay the hospitality by allowing the priest to enjoy an erection when watching my brother have a bath – as long as it did not go too far in his direction – and he seems to have managed the situation with the utmost tact and diplomacy. The don was a different kettle of fish. My brother was frightened of nothing, but the strain of keeping him beyond even arm's length was very tiring, and the boredom of the holidays spent with him stultifying.

John was once embroiled in an argument with my father about the Wolfenden Report and the inevitable perverted orgies which must follow it, and reminded my father of the risks of corruption to which he had unwittingly, my brother politely presumed, exposed him.

My father was cornered. He could not plead ignorance of a simple, universally acknowledged, psychological fact of life because when either of us has ever discussed psychology with him and dared to suggest that on even one, isolated point, we might, just possibly, be better informed than he was, we were assured that this was not the case. My father was an authority –

the authority – he had to be. His positions demanded a close study of psychology – so detailed and in such depth that it was quite clear that something was amiss in the medical world. Conferences, seminars and assemblies of psychologists did not gather at his feet for further study and sit-ins. As usual, though, he emerged from his corner with the answer: Yes, he said, it had been a terrible thing to do, and the mental torture, the anguish, the agony of having to do it still haunted him, but he had been forced to accept the invitations because of our mother who (voice shaking with emotion) would have had a nervous breakdown if he had had to alert her to the existence of *The Vice* at all!

Strangely, it never occurred to him to protect my mother and my brother with the tiniest white lie, "Not really a good idea to send the boy off to stay with bachelors – one doesn't know what the cooking arrangements are," for instance.

Stranger still, my mother told us both at the time that she hated my brother going to stay with those men – there was something she didn't "quite like" about them.

⁂

Sex education was not on the curriculum when I was at school. The facts of life may have been delicately hinted at, or even openly described with pornographic diagrams titillatingly displayed on the blackboard in Science lessons.

However, at my first Biology lesson I was confronted with a dead cockroach preserved in methylated spirit. When I told my mother she 'got me out of Science' for the rest of my schooldays. She treasured 'getting me out of things' and, on the basis that one good turn deserves another, I had to persuade myself to take exception to activities which, looking back, in reality I rather enjoyed. That involved very confusing double, triple standards of behaviour, convincing myself that I did not like something, telling her, getting myself 'excused,' and repressing feelings of envy for the girls doing the things I did-didn't want to do. Finally, falling into the trap of hating a perfectly satisfactory school because she, while letting me stay there, tirelessly indoctrinated me with the notion that it was a bad school that was, she told me, giving me an inferiority complex. Given a reasonable chance, that school just might have helped me. The headmistresses of Wychwood were Miss Lea and Miss Coster who enjoyed a lesbian relationship as well as teaching. Miss Coster was unusually enlightened for the time, and I remember quite a number of girls, including a kleptomaniac to whom we had to be kind when extracting our stolen pencil boxes from her desk, a cretin who ate snails during the mid-morning break, a number of emotionally deprived children deposited there by Empire-propping parents for school holidays as well as terms, and even girls whose fathers, for reasons other than absence abroad, death or divorce, did not exist.

I suspect that there must have been mothers who geared

themselves up to giving their daughters at least some inkling of what lay in store for them with approaching menstruation. Not mine. On the contrary, she often told us how her mother had been so fastidious that she had never been seen even going in or out of the lavatory. As my mother was one of ten children, I am awe-struck at the sheer genius with which my grandmother must have achieved such an astonishing feat. John lazily accepted the easy answer – that our grandmother died at the age of eighty of what must have been a very uncomfortable, lingering illness, namely years of constipation and non-passing of water.

I remember the appalling guilt which swept over me when, as very small children, we were called in to lunch one day just as John was demonstrating to me the force and length of the spout of water he could make against the neighbour's fence at the end of the garden. At the age of six he informed me, completely convincingly, that babies were made by fathers forcing mothers to drink their husbands' fountains, and I was haunted by a fantasy of my mother submissively kneeling in front of my father in the role of a neighbour's unwilling human fence. When we asked my mother how babies came she said gloomily that we would know when we were older but she added, more optimistically, I might never need to find out.

The onset of my periods was threatened, in traditional fashion, by three schoolgirls. One told us that she and her mother bathed together except, of course – meaningful look – when her mother was unable to. I was absolutely dumbfounded at the thought of a naked mother. The idea that my mother undressed had never crossed my mind. I suppose if the poser had been posed I would have protested, for after all I protected her too, that she went to bed fully clothed and, in her magical, marvellous, mysterious way, reappeared in the morning in different clothes.

However, that was only the first shock in store for me. Another girl with the nonchalant know-all air of a thirteen-year-old, said: "Oh, you mean once a month when she is bleeding wee-wee worms?" Suspecting that I was being tormented and teased – I often was – I said, "You're telling stories. I don't believe people bleed wee-wee worms."

Reality had to be faced. The well-developed third girl invited me into the cloakroom with her and proved that she, for one, was afflicted with that catastrophic curse.

I put it right out of my mind. Owing to undernourishment, I was physically underdeveloped, and although my contemporaries one by one joined the ranks of girls "excused" from games, gym, and dancing at regular intervals (a knowing look between them and the schoolmistress was enough to be 'excused'), it slowly dawned on me that there was truth behind the fearful stories of "the curse." I didn't think it would happen to me and, for a long – well – period, I was right. Long after all my friends were regularly escaping netball and lacrosse – and I could sniff compensation there – I was still perfectly 'well.'

When I was nearly seventeen I was caught at school, mid-morning, unprotected and ashamed. I went home to lunch and it took every ounce of courage to tell my mother. Fuel was added to the fire of my adoration of her by her reaction. It was all right! She had not told me herself in case it frightened me, but girls did have it and, though I must expect discomfort and pain, which in due course I dutifully endured, it was best not to mention it to anyone. She had been expecting it and was prepared. She warmed a sanitary towel in front of the hissing gas fire in her bedroom and, at that moment, I remembered Lally having a day in bed during the previous holidays and how anxiously I had awaited her death: surely such whisperings, hush-hushing and general distraction of the attention from me could only be caused by its imminence. It must have been an intensely tricky day for my mother. My sister had to be sworn to secrecy and I had to be kept out of the way. Strange little parcels wrapped in lavatory paper were surreptitiously popped into the incinerator and my mother's evasiveness about what was happening was overtly, purposely, sinister.

Now it was my turn. I assumed, but had to make sure, that she would not tell my father. But the heady scent of another neurosis to be smothered with love was irresistible. "I'm afraid he'll have to know," she said. I couldn't see why, but she explained that it meant I was grown-up, and it was, therefore, a very important development. I was rooted to the hearthrug. Not only had I got the curse but also, suddenly, in the middle of an ordinary weekday morning, I had grown up. That meant the daunting responsibilities my father had said grown-ups had to bear would be mine. On my shoulders I should have to carry the burden of overdrafts, bills, house maintenance, education, and possibly even scaffolding. Even I, even then, did not actually think I would have scaffolding on my body though, now I come to think of it, it might have supported the hump.

But whenever the tiles blew off the roof, which they did at the slightest puff of wind in the dismal Victorian mansion in which we then lived, my father became more than usually morose anticipating the phenomenal expense of scaffolding.

My mother was always right, of course, but the paralysing embarrassment of feeling wee-wee worms oozing out of me when my father came home and knowing that he knew they were and, furthermore, would shortly be thrusting bills, overdrafts and mortgages at me, was petrifying. Fortunately, there was a long gap before I was 'unwell' again and then the pain was so dagger-like that I retired to bed, thus ensuring that I did innocently cultivate the maximum physical discomfort and, coincidentally, keep out of his way. Except, of course, on dancing class days when, well padded to absorb the pent-up flood, I was free of pain; and possibly one of the few girls in the school never to take the opportunity of being "off colour" for dancing.

Something had to be done with me, though. Or, rather, I had to do something. But what? Lally had failed School Certificate, but ropes were pulled by my father who, quite rightly, thought it unfair, at any rate in her case, that passing School Certificate depended on passing mathematics. If you failed mathematics and achieved distinctions in everything else, you had still failed. For her, in spite of a total lack of distinction in any subject, the ropes were pulled so hard that she was admitted to Bedford Physical Training College. I was naturally expected to fail every paper, and the fact that I had passed with distinctions in all the English subjects and Latin somehow escaped notice. And my father even bestowed a gift on me.

Along with a remarkably perceptive Latin teacher, who appeared to be blithely oblivious of my imbecility, he coached me in Latin – and a very good coach he was. Apart from having to be in the same room with him, even chaperoned as I was by my mother, I enjoyed his lessons and easily wrote a play in Latin, which was performed at the end-of-the-school-year jamboree. What is surprising is that he took so little credit for this modest success that he did not bother to come to the actual performance and take a bow.

True, it was all my own work but it astounds me that he let me get away with it. It was the highest spot of a school career exceptional solely for my breaking the record of non-attendance. I still have my school reports, and the lowest number of days absence I achieved in any term was twenty-five.

※

Even while I was at school my father called me a social parasite. In those days teenagers from our social background did not augment their pocket money by doing paper rounds, delivering Christmas mail or working in shops on Saturdays, so I was only one of hoards of social parasites, but he certainly hammered the point home that it was a disreputable thing to be.

John and I needed to augment our pocket money and my father offered to pay us a halfpenny per bucket full of stones picked out of the gravel path-surrounded grass. One old penny between us for two buckets full of stones. Assuming that one halfpenny then might even have been worth ten new pence now, it was still a formidable task for so little reward. We toiled away for a whole morning, by the end of which we had earned a farthing between us. John was all for nicking a few from the path but I knew that my father's all-seeing eye, though at that moment otherwise engaged, would spot cheating the second he arrived home. Slave labour was not our metier and, sadly, we resigned ourselves to continued poverty.

I suppose the mechanism behind my father's behaviour is easily explained. He himself, as an undergraduate, had supported out of his scholarship money, an eccentric, loveable, roguish solicitor-father and mother. My grandfather was not struck-off for embezzlement or dishonesty. Oddly, he was not struck off at all, but word got round that, though enchanting, he was not an entirely reliable advisor and, from the giddy heights of owning two houses and a private yacht, he quickly descended, unemployed, into a tiny cottage in the wilds of Buckinghamshire. As a student, my father was reputed to have lived exclusively on porridge. His elder brothers may or may not have helped to shoulder the burden of supporting impecunious parents, but my father had the strongest sense of duty. On leaving Oxford, he passed into the Civil Service among the top six applicants. All very laudable, but basing his own success in life on the hardships he had had to suffer resulted in even greater hardships for us. John did not win a scholarship to Oxford and was given rather less than the meagre minimum allowance officially recommended for Commoners.

Having left school, my father decided that it was time I left home. I was not consulted and at the beginning of the autumn term, I found myself in Worcester where Lally was teaching Gymnastics, Games, PT and Eurhythmics very successfully at the Alice Ottley School. I was to help (unpaid) in the kindergarten, teaching children to tie their shoelaces.

A bed-sitting room had been found for me by Lally in a small house in Malvern belonging to an AA scout who was away in the army. The sitting part of my room consisted of an orange and blue striped canvas deck chair. My father paid for the room, bed and breakfast.

He arranged an allowance of £12 a year, deposited in the Bank, for clothes, toiletries, fares to and from Malvern to the Alice Ottley School in Worcester and Worcester to Oxford if I wanted a weekend at home. The children bored me beyond description but far, far worse than that was the quite serious hunger pangs I felt by the end of each afternoon. Lunch was provided at the school, but I could not afford to buy anything more and pay the fare to and from Worcester. My solution was to stand outside a Cadena Café, sniffing the appetising smell of coffee and rolls while smoking Craven A cigarettes, which, on an empty stomach, made me feel too sick to eat.

About half-way through the term help arrived. I had been exceedingly friendly in Oxford, just before I left school, with a medical student in his thirties. We met at a dance and I imagined I was in love. His first words to me were, "Our eyes met across a crowded room" which I thought very romantic. He was from Argentina and was up at Trinity College, but for some unspecified (to me) crime had been "gated" for the rest of the Michaelmas Term. My father had forbidden me to see him in Oxford. The head of his college had warned my father that he was an "unsavoury character". Part of his charm may have been his sports car in which he met me at the school with a shudder each day. His name was Alec Macgregor and he chose a hotel in Malvern in which to spend the enforced time out of Oxford. He appreciated my cynical sense of humour and rescued me from the one and only time in my life when I had experienced real hunger. He took care of me for the rest of my time at the school, during which I had no contact with Lally apart from being allowed to attend her Eurhythmics class.

My teaching career was shown to be appreciated by a leaving present from Miss Roden, the headmistress, of a heavy book with the enticing title, *Guide to Worcester*.

※

It was decided that I should attend a domestic science course for a year, at the end of which no diplomas or certificates were bestowed. Quite rightly. It was what was called a Bride's Course. Its aim was to teach the students how to dispose of unwanted husbands by slow starvation or even straightforward poisoning. It was geared to meet the needs of the aristocracy and we were taught how much scrag-end of mutton per head should be bought for the below-stairs staff, how to supervise the fashioning of double-damask table napkins into water-lilies and, very occasionally, how to cook something exotic – so that your cook would know you knew as much as she did. I spent a whole week on a galantine of beef welded together with aspic and garnished with hard-boiled eggs painstakingly moulded into – yes – water lilies. I expect some students were taught how to braise goldfish to go with all those water lilies with which the tables of the upper classes must be awash. By the time my galantine was finished, it had a sinister greenish tinge and smelt of cheese.

The warden, Meg Buchanan, was a Scot and, like some other Scottish women I have met, after their initial dislike of me, they suddenly latch onto what they think is a kind of *Embodiment of Southern Eccentricity* and, when they do, they double up with mirth and cries of "Och aye, ye are a one" before I even speak. The warden was one of these perceptive ladies. I was very fond of her and we spent more time having wee drams of this and that in her study than I did at the stove the whole year I was there.

As I was still stage-struck, my father decided that there was music "in the family". Not, of course, my brother's music. John dabbled in enough history to get him a degree at Oxford, while concentrating almost exclusively on composing. Having my voice trained would be allowable. Week after week I warbled away to a singing master, Arthur Cranmer, who arranged an audition for me with the trainer of singers from Glyndebourne. He listened to me sing and said he would take me on. The snag was that I hated singing. I never had a good voice, but I suppose it must have been passable for me to be accepted. After one or two trips to London, I found the train journey too exhausting and my mother saved me from yet another possible flight to freedom. I don't blame her. It was mad of me to miss attempting to do anything even on the fringe of what I wanted, and I would have dashed off to Russia to dance without a backward glance, but I never would have enjoyed singing and no one would have appreciated being sung at by me. The original singing master groped me in the lift to his room, which was another reason for giving it up.

The inevitable next step was a secretarial course, which was run by a snob out of the bottom of the bottom drawer. She thought it unseemly for girls of my background to mix with 'common' girls who would have to earn their livings. So we six 'nice' girls were segregated in one room and had a Pitman's shorthand book and a couple of elderly typewriters assigned to us, while the other twenty embryo secretaries were crowded into a smaller room and were actively, personally, taught. The head joined us for our mid-morning break, picking up a bit of free elocution, and apart from that, we never saw her. I did that course with a friend, Geneste Beaton who had learnt to turn dining-room tables into water-lily ponds with me and we can still write *Dear Sir* and *Yours Faithfully* in shorthand.

However, I did, years later, have a brilliant three-year career as Confidential Secretary to an actor. I met him at a party and he was, that evening, acting with great aplomb the tragic part of a *Star without a Secretary*. Toppling piles of fan mail waited to be answered, unwanted callers with no one suitable to turn them away and the ceaseless, nerve-wracking ringing of the telephone bell were driving him berserk. Someone had to be found to deal with all this, not to mention the embarrassing requests to open fêtes, charity bazaars, adorn balls and attend royal premieres. I took pity on him and my unemployed self, and offered my services.

If I had had only to answer fan mail, ten minutes a year would have been more than enough time. Character actors are not the matinee idols of the film world, and in the three years I worked for him he received approximately four fan letters a year. The calls to open village fairs were non-existent, but I was kept fully occupied shopping for his wife, writing out breathtakingly vast cheques for them to sign and ferrying the children to and from their various schools.

From the work point of view, it was the dullest job I've ever had, except for eighteen months as a cleaning lady. I was a status symbol. I could hardly bear to drag myself away. That family could not live without drama. His work was nothing at all compared with the scenes enacted in the home. Staff were engaged to be sacked within hours for stealing, insanity or simply because the appalling ugliness of their faces had escaped notice at the interviews when they were engaged.

I have it straight from the horse's mouth that there is not a single actor who has not got a drink problem, marital trouble, lack of talent, VD, or all four together. Couples I had known for years, I was told, had gone on holiday together as families, the result being that no one was sure whose child belonged to which father. A solicitor in the town was struck off the books in London and had to come out to the provinces to practice! Sometimes the family were on speaking terms with each other, sometimes they were having punch-ups. I never knew whether I was going to be met with a "Hello, darling – Isn't she gorgeous today?" or an icy "Good Morning. Two cheques were not made out yesterday, and the agent's letter has been lost."

I was accused of embezzlement, stealing stamps and the outdated guarantee of the Rolls Royce and, if they had not been so mad, I would have taken it seriously and been hurt. As it was, I took the immense sum of five shillings an hour they paid me, which very nearly covered the use they made of my car, equably accepted their treatment of me and, being a Confidential Secretary, bore with fortitude the agonising temptation which had to be avoided of entertaining my friends with stories of their antics. They all needed me to polarize their loves and hates and act as a full-time appreciative audience.

They would charm and repel within minutes and, on the whole, I enjoyed it, but the time came when they were in Hollywood and on their return, I was accused of signing cheques without the co-signature of their solicitor and I was sacked.

༶

Having learnt how to turn dinner tables into lily ponds and to top and tail letters with shorthand Dear Sir and Yours Faithfully, I was persuaded by various friends to apply for a job in MI5, which had been moved out of London to the safety of Blenheim Palace at Woodstock. Applying to work for the Secret Service required no qualifications other than a high-class accent and appearance, so my interview passed without a hitch. I signed the Official Secrets Act, had a passport photo stuck onto a yellow card with red stripes and was ready to help win the war. There had been a fire in MI5, which had destroyed a number of files before the office had moved to Woodstock but lists of the files had survived. I was in Section 9 (known as Destruction). My task was to type the names from the lists onto green cards, which then had to be slotted into the right places in the filing cupboards. This took six months. The head of the section oversaw this vital war work, decided it was not vital enough and I was put in sole charge of moving the cards to waste paper bins.

After Section 9, I was moved to R4, where we dealt with real, very thick files holding huge amounts of papers all labelled 'Personal File,' with a number. I had to read the files, which might take an hour or two, extract what I judged to be the pith of the information therein and transfer it on to *Complete Information Cards* about the size of half an A5 piece of paper. I was very soon known as the CIC Queen as a result of being a fast reader with a talent for picking out important details from these vast amounts of paper. Disregarding the *Official Secrets Act,* I can reveal that the information in these files consisted of dates of birth, addresses, any distinguishing features, occupation and, most important, *Member of the British Union of Fascists* or *The Communist Party* and police records. Most of the staff were housed for the duration in Keble College, but I, of course, lived at home where my father charged me for my board and lodging. We worked seven days a week, including Christmas, Easter and all other holidays. We could choose one day off a week. I very seldom chose Sundays and never Christmas when my father would be free. Thus I won the Second World War.

Towards the end of the war, I met a man whose defects had never been noticed for the simple reason that he never came to the house. Instinct must have preserved me from making my usual mistake. He came from Yorkshire where, as we all know, a great deal of scrubbing and baking goes on, but somehow on his way southwards he lost some of the mental toughness that life up there requires. He also acquired a sense of humour and wit that just passes muster north of the Wash as a regrettable but bearable momentary touch of insanity.

I met Geoffrey Hobson, unoriginally, at a dance. He had a magnetic personality, was a natural dancer and scintillatingly witty. We scintillated at each other. He had been reading Modern Languages at Cambridge when he was conscripted into the Intelligence Corps. When I first knew him, he was on a course at Oriel College learning, among other things, how to interrogate German prisoners of war. I do not believe that British soldiers are kinder, more civilised than soldiers of other nationalities. Given the circumstances under which atrocities are likely to be committed they will commit them as brutally as the rest of the world's population. I don't think Geoffrey would have, being more global than patriotic in outlook. He had, in fact, considered registering as a pacifist but his elder brother, his only sibling, had been killed early in the war and perhaps that was the swaying factor against pacifism for him. Anyway, there he was in Oxford learning to interrogate.

One of the less unpleasant things he had to do was to interrogate in fancy dress. German prisoners were terrified of Polish officers and spilt the beans much faster confronted by a Polish officer's uniform and questioned in German spoken with a Polish accent.

The course lasted several weeks, weeks during which the sun never set for me. The moment when I knew for certain that he would be the one not to be 'turned away' came when he invited me to go to a cricket match in which he was playing. He had played cricket for Cambridge and he took the game seriously. I appeared in the middle of his innings; he caught sight of me and gently, deliberately, tipped the ball into the hands of the nearest fielder. He did not even want to watch the end of the match, and his lack of team spirit weighted the last ounce of the scales in his favour for me. We wandered off and snuggled up together in the long grass surrounding the pitch.

"Pure gold," I thought, as the sun glinted in his curly brown hair. "Pure gold," I thought as khaki-coloured eyes gazed into mine. "I love him."

"I love you," we said together.

Soon after that he was posted abroad and, for the first of three times, left me bereft. Oddly, although he was in the front line and although I knew there was always more than a chance that he might be parachuted into enemy territory as a spy, I never feared for his safety. There are spin-off benefits from neuroses. Love equals safety. And he was so strong that no Nazi jackals could hurt him. He was God and, like my father, omnipotent – but a tender God – a God who was on my side.

He wrote endlessly, daily at least, and while other girls waited and waited for letters we were extraordinarily lucky. Our mail was never held up for more than a day or two. I wrote too, twice a day at least and often in the night. Perhaps the very bulk of our correspondence defeated censors and gave it the appearance of being top-priority documents. In one of the hundreds of letters he wrote to me, he said that Romeo and Juliet and Caesar and Cleopatra had lived in states of unrelieved hostility compared with the life that lay ahead of us.

Eleven months later he arrived in England without warning, but I felt him coming. I had arranged to go to a dance that night and out of the blue, at five o'clock in the evening, I knew that I must stay at home. Not only have I always had a tyrannical social conscience which forbids me to let people down, but also, of course, nothing short of a major crisis would normally prevent me dancing. At five o'clock I rang up one of my friends, said I had a headache and could not come. I amazed myself. At five-thirty, Geoffrey, whom I believed to be in Holland, rang up from Harwich to say he was in England. I had had three letters, posted in Holland, from him that morning. It must surely have been telepathy. He would be arriving at midnight. I told my mother that I was going to meet him at the station and from that moment she went into a steep decline. She warned me that I would tire myself out staying up so late and if he was determined to come at once he should find a hotel for the night and I should go to bed and wait until the morning to see him.

I waited and waited for that late, late train to arrive. He stepped out of it, I was in his arms and it was as though we had never been separated. We sat up nearly all night, drinking the champagne he had brought with him, talking, talking, kissing, talking and kissing again and again. We decided to get married by special licence that week.

My parents had visitors, Eric and Alice Bamford, for the weekend and if that efficient strong-minded woman visitor had not been there I do not know how we could have achieved it. I had no trousseau – not that it mattered – but in effect I had no parents either. My mother's decline was so steep that she vanished from the scene and took refuge in her bedroom and my father was, as always, so immersed in running Oxford University, that he took no interest in any of us except that, as a time-saver, he did allow Alice to make, within tight financial limits, arrangements for a small lunch-party after the wedding ceremony and bully him into attending both. She also buckled to and telephoned clergymen, sorted out my clothes, packed for me and made appointments. We did everything else.

Geoffrey chose for his Best Man a delightful journalist, Stanley Parker, who had always given me good publicity on the local paper.

Stanley and his brother, Kenneth, were both gay, and so devoted to each other that it was rumoured that they were incestuous. They were also adoring satellites of an enormous, red-brick edifice of a mother who could often be seen toppling waveringly along the streets, slightly tipsy, her sons, one each side of her, acting as crutches as she ricocheted from one to the other.

Stanley was a show-stealing, charming Best Man, but there was a moment of anxiety when he was seeing us off to London for the start of a four-day honeymoon and he embraced and kissed Geoffrey for so long I began to wonder whether he or I were the bride. Geoffrey had insisted that we visit my doctor to make sure that, in our hurry, condoms would be safe enough contraceptives for the moment. We need not have done. My doctor examined me and found that I was impenetrable and would have to have an operation for which there was no time. It was mortifying, and I was furious with myself for not having had it all dealt with before. It would have been a bit of a mess though, because I was flooded by an early period starting on the morning of our wedding.

When I went to the bathroom that night, I locked the door. Geoffrey was astonished and gently insisted that he must be allowed in. I was embarrassed by the soiled sanitary towel flung carelessly in the corner. He saw me glance at it. "It's alright, you know," he said. "I even love it."

Our four-day honeymoon was a mixture of ecstasy and misery. Unevenly, ecstatic days and sleepless, miserable nights. John had spent many hours, during our adolescence, persuading me not only that sex was a good thing, but that girls as well as men enjoyed it and had a right to do so. In a sense, those four nights might not have been such a misery if he had not bothered. I might have resigned myself to taking Mrs Baldwin's advice to her niece "to lie back and think of the Empire."

As a small child, my first visual experience of the sexual act had been the sight of a dog mounting a bitch in the road outside the house. Innocently, I had drawn my mother's attention to the dogs playing and, flushed with embarrassment, she had forbidden me to watch. The dogs were being "Ugh! Disgusting." Later that day, 'something nasty happened in the bicycle shed.' John told me what game those awful dogs had been playing. Furthermore, he, figuratively, pressed home the point by telling me that he could, if I wished, do it to me and the result would be that I would have a baby. I refused to co-operate, thus depriving the press of startling headlines.

SIX-YEAR-OLD GIRL GIVES BIRTH TO BABY. NAMES BROTHER AS FATHER OF INFANT.

I was desperately anxious that Geoffrey, at least, should enjoy his honeymoon.

"Don't worry about me," I implored. "I'm sure you can get in and I don't care how much it hurts." Apart from a visit to a brothel in Italy, he had been faithful to me during the eleven months of our engagement. Very much against his better judgement he had a bash – and bash it was – and, as he bashed, the vision of those sex-maniac dogs came back to me. I hated it. By the middle of the morning each day, the traumatic experiences of the night before dissolved and I was as randy as he was. Now and again, I would swoop momentarily into black depression. Time was so short, he would be deserting me and I felt trapped in a situation, a honeymoon, a marriage, which should be a fulfilling experience and I would have to go home unfulfilled, unhappy, unsure, and act the part of the radiant bride. Furthermore, I was to have an operation involving ten days in the gynaecological department of a nursing home. I doubted my ability to pass it off as a jaunty little escapade for the removal of tonsils or appendix.

It is difficult to decide whether I simply rose to the occasion, whether the warm welcome of my friends coupled with sympathy for my grass-widowhood and mysterious indisposition, whether the constant flow of love-letters, deliveries of red roses on the 13th of each month (the date of our wedding) always accompanied by a hand-written message from him – with typical foresight he had scribbled them out in a florists' and ordered them to be delivered, monthly, before leaving me – or the fact that the dreaded parting had been softened with such reassuring tenderness by him, but I did appear radiant, and remember only the yearning for him I felt at the time.

In June he reappeared again, out of the blue, without warning, for a three-week honeymoon. Having had the operation, it was going to be all right this time. We went to London, Cambridge and finally back to a hotel in Oxford for the last day or two. The three-week deadline in which I had to reach an orgasm, many orgasms, oppressed me. The more oppressed and anxious I became, the less the chances of gratification, and my anxiety became so obsessive that much of the time was spent crying. He kept promising me that, in the end, everything would come right – he always chose words with care – until one morning, before I was really awake, I felt him looking at me.

Before the tensions could take over, he took me. Slowly, tenderly and soothingly he made love to me and after he had caressed and loved me to the point of no return and my climax was over, I remember thinking to myself: "I have come home," at which moment he said, "I have woken my sleeping Princess."

W.W. and Maude Mary (*née* Rootham) Veale. Parents of Douglas Veale.

Douglas, Evelyn, Janet and John Veale.

Margaret (known as Lally) at Ducks Hill Road, Northwood.

Douglas and Evelyn Veale at Ducks Hill Road.

Janet and John on the terrace at Danbury, Ducks Hill Road, Northwood, Middlesex.

Janet and John Veale.

Lally, Janet and John Veale. Seaside holiday in Devon.

Douglas, Evelyn, Janet and John Veale on holiday in Cornwall.

Margaret McCallum (*née* Veale): "Lally".

Geoffrey Hamilton Hobson on engagement to Janet.

When war ended, Geoffrey had arrived home with rheumatic fever, contracted while occupying Holland. Having served without a day's sick leave throughout the last two years of the war, when he was taken ill he was accused of malingering, and passed fit for further service. After the malingering diagnosis had had to be abandoned because he could only move from A to B by commanding a German police dog he had looted in Holland to drag him to and fro, he was shunted about from hospital to hospital and, finally, shipped home to England to what had been temporarily converted from a Mental into a Military hospital near Epsom. There we spent some of the happiest days of our marriage. He had a padded cell to himself; the sister was the epitome of the gentle, dove-like woman usually constrained to falling in love with a handsome doctor. The doctors were clever and the hospital so short-staffed that I was allowed to stay in the ward, eat with the nurses, look after Geoffrey and when he was asleep, help look after the other patients. There was one wizened, white-haired, skeleton of a man whom I took to be between sixty and seventy. He was so weak he could not feed himself and I used to spoon soup and custard into him. I discovered he was forty-one. He had been on the Burma Road as a prisoner of war of the Japanese.

However, the thought of me alone and helpless in Darkest Surrey preyed on my mother's mind.

It would have preyed even more insistently had she known of one incident which occurred when Geoffrey's condition improved and I no longer needed to sleep in the hospital and moved into a hotel in Epsom.

One very dark, foggy night I missed the last bus into the town. It was much too far to walk and I waved down a passing motorist. The driver was the prototype of the mythical sinister commercially travelling, coarse rapist on the lookout for victims, but I was much too delighted at finding transport to notice and would not have recognised that kind of danger even if I had been aware of its existence.

True to form he turned up a lane, stopped the car, dragged me towards him and panted, moist lips searching for mine, "What do I get for this, ducky?" while pushing a fat hot hand up my leg, under my skirt. "Nothing," I said, struggling away from him. He persisted, very roughly. "Please," I implored. "I'm exhausted. I have been nursing my husband, who is very ill, all day at the hospital. I'm too tired to fight you. PLEASE, just PLEASE, let me go," I burst into tears and fumbled for the handle of the door.

"Oh, my God!" he said. "Oh, my God! Oh, I'm sorry. Oh, I do beg your pardon, dearie. Where is it that you want to go?" That potentially nasty little man was truly remorseful. He started up the car again and drove me to the very door of my hotel. He sat so far away from me that I think, had I asked, he would have pushed the car the whole way. I have often thought of him since, with gratitude and surprise. Lurking beneath that lascivious exterior was a humane man, a man with compassion and kindness. We talked all the way to Epsom. I am sure that, had I not been honestly, genuinely, desperately worried and tired, he would not have been so easily thwarted. I doubt if the incident turned over a new leaf in his life. He was so obviously accustomed to deftly getting what he could when and where opportunities arose. But he befriended me on an occasion when I had to have a friend, and I hope his better nature has not been put to the test and traded upon too many times since.

⁂

My mother persuaded my father to pull some of his many strings, (it seemed that the world was populated exclusively by puppets prancing helplessly, mechanically, to the forceful jerking of my father's string-pulling) and get us moved out of our little padded love-nest to Oxford where I, at least, could be properly looked after by her.

Geoffrey agreed to the move on one condition: that I should

be allowed unrestricted visiting. It seemed a reasonable request since the staff at the hospital had generously and repeatedly said that I had saved his life. My father assured us that he would arrange it all – and not only that, instead of a padded cell Geoffrey would have a private room. We sadly but confidently left our haven in a vast, glass ambulance – there was to be none of that uncomfortable bouncing about in a St. John's one for me, my mother saw to that – accompanied by a young doctor, Dr Toye, sent, I think, for the ride as his only contribution to my husband's welfare on the journey was to ask me if and when pills should be consumed. I handed my husband over to the Radcliffe Infirmary in Oxford, and with Dr Toye, nipped home for lunch. Two hours later, when I visited Geoffrey – who a famous heart specialist called into the other hospital for consultations, Dr East, had ordered should be propped, day and night, in a sitting position – was flat on his back, struggling for breath, in a public ward. It was, the little black-eyed, black-hearted sister told me, a rule of the hospital that all patients should lie down until examined by a doctor. "Then why has no doctor been sent for?" I asked. Not the way to appease the Queen of the ward. "This is Tuesday," she continued, "and visiting hours are from 3pm to 4pm on Wednesdays and 2.30pm to 4.30pm on Saturdays and Sundays. You should not be here."

I had learnt to lift Geoffrey alone, so I lifted him then and there at Oxford, sat on his sandbag of a pillow and as he leant against me felt his breathing ease. I was quite prepared to fight the sister to the death – hers – and nearly did. I once saw her outside the hospital waiting for a bus and with regrettable restraint refrained from pushing her under it.

At last, a young intern whom John and I seemed to have known forever – he had been sitting and failing his examinations for so long – arrived in the ward and I told him my husband's case history and how to treat the immediate crisis.

Once John was having a drink in the pub opposite the hospital when that tardy intern came in with a friend. Said one to the other:

"It's perfectly simple really. Nothing to worry about at all."

The friend: " It sounds very complicated to me."

"Good heavens no! Nothing to it! You open it up and wait for the red, seething mess to die down a bit, " John was riveted, "then you see a kind of blackish lump," John felt slightly faint, "and, by then you should be able to get near enough to hoik it out. There's a special sort of tong affair with long handles they throw in," John, gasping heard, "for extracting the clinker. One advantage is that you can run a couple of radiators off it as well."

I also informed the sister that I would be visiting my husband all day and every day while he was in hospital. The misunderstanding over the visiting was not her fault. She was as much the victim of my father's inflated ego as I was, but after the initial fencing she did behave with considerably less grace than I did. I used to wait for anything up to half an hour,

Geoffrey and I mouthing messages to each other in the sluice-lined passage leading to his bed, to ask ingratiatingly for permission to step into 'Her Ward', while she passed, brushing against me, over and over again, determinedly refusing to catch my eye. She had missed her vocation as a waitress in a sleazy café.

※

Eventually there was a crisis. I visited one day to find Geoffrey panting, relapsed, having been "examined" by no less than ten "doctors" in an hour. I complained to the intern who had so sensibly improved his chances of passing at least one of his examinations first go by taking my advice on the treatment of certain rheumatic fever complications. He told me that it was of invaluable help to have the opinion of the ten doctors. I replied acidly that we were quite satisfied with the opinion of Professor Witts, the Professor of Clinical Medicine in charge of my husband's case and that the medical students who had risked my husband's life would have to endanger people for whom I cared less in the future. Geoffrey was mysteriously moved, overnight, to the Private Block, but not without one last battle for me. I was sent for, SENT FOR, by Matron. The message that I was to report to her office at 3 o'clock precisely the next day was delivered to me by a probationer. I ought ruthlessly to have sent the probationer back with the answer that the day and time were inconvenient and that I would contact Matron in the unlikely event of my wanting to meet her outside her ward rounds, when the nurses and I stood, and the patients lay, to attention. However, I was young and naïve and I dutifully joined a queue of apprehensive nurses outside her office, punctually at 3 o'clock the next day.

When my turn of the mat came it was like reports of meetings with Hitler. What seemed like miles of carpet lay between the door and her desk. She did not look up when I entered. She was perusing, before signing, papers. Lists of names of nurses, patients and patients' relatives to be horsewhipped, tarred and feathered in public? I ploughed my way across the room and after several minutes she glared at me and I impudently sat down, uninvited, without permission, opposite her desk. She stared coldly at me in silence while tapping the desk with a pencil. No butterflies fluttered in my stomach in time to the tapping. I calmly sat and waited for her harangue to start. I disliked her, knew it and was not scared. She carefully rearranged her blotting pad, put down the pencil and spoke.

Ever since our arrival in this hospital, our behaviour had, it appeared, caused the virtual disruption of the entire institution. Even the recovery of the other patients was in serious jeopardy owing to our refusal to obey rules designed for their well-being. In fact, the other patients in the ward benefited from my visits and said so. Our carefree disregard of the precise angles in the folds at the ends of bedspreads, the vital necessity for preserving the required length of visible sheet, and the involvement of the other men in our giggles and conversations, had led to one or two wholesome mutinies among them. Deprived of their own visitors for days at a time, they enjoyed the crumbs of attention we scattered round the ward and, while mostly devoted to the young nurses, they dared to ignore some of sister's sillier rules. I assume that the patients I was recklessly risking slaughtering were in other wards which I had neither the time nor the inclination to visit. "Geoffrey was only a lieutenant," Matron told me, "but a colonel had died on a Friday *without seeing his wife* because *she* had had the self-discipline not to try to visit him outside official visiting hours." It was reminiscent of the reading-aloud lie because her parting shot was that my father, who was a member of the governing body of the hospital, would be horrified when she reported it all to him. And she knew what he would have to say to me. I was speechless: because she simply left me no time to answer before commanding me to leave her room.

Some years later, much to my glee, the doctors belatedly ganged up against that loathsome woman and, not without appeals to the governing body, the regional hospital board and the Minister of Health, meticulously and rivetingly reported in the national press, she was prematurely retired. Possibly with a *Golden Handshake* – but, nevertheless, deprived of her post, forced to resign, sacked.

Our arrival in the Private Wing was like stepping out of a prison into the Ritz. The sister, humane, warm-hearted and charming, insisted that I visit my husband as often as I possibly could. I was always welcome, had my clothes admired and advice on theirs sought by the nurses, and, to crown it all, Geoffrey's health improved so much that he could sit out of bed, then walk, then dress, and finally come out of hospital altogether for whole afternoons and evenings. But fate, ever at action stations to rush in reinforcements to flatten me when life flowed too smoothly, had a secret weapon up its sleeve. Geoffrey got too well. He was fit enough to go to a convalescent home for officers and the hospital could keep a bed for him no longer. He was sent to a Country House Convalescent Home to recover completely. He was warned by Professor Witts not to be afraid of being thought to molly-coddle himself if he continued to rest in the afternoons, relinquished all strenuous activities and resigned himself to behaving like the hypochondriac he wasn't for one more year. Much against my mother's wishes, I went with him and stayed in a pub in the village.

The Home was run by an aged doctor and matron who administered it haphazardly and jovially from what we thought was a rather booze-ridden little flatlet. They had been resurrected for the war from the Red Cross or the grave, I forget which. They obviously liked us but thought we needed pepping up. Over scones, tea and a swig from the gin bottle I was warned that we were becoming a bit neurotic about my husband's health. They hit the nail squarely on the head regarding me – I was neurotic about everything – but Geoffrey suffered from a feckless lack of neuroses. He took their advice, braced himself up, played clock golf and croquet in the afternoons, progressed to ping-pong and, very soon, to cross-country runs. To his fury, he started flagging, forgotten symptoms returned and he asked for a medical board, every soldier's right. They talked him out of it, and he duly collapsed into hospital again, where, to the outspoken fury of our Professor, he died quite unnecessarily and in indescribable pain. Added to which, he died, inconsiderately, in the middle of my father's annual summer holiday.

༄

To me, Geoffrey's death symbolised abandonment and the deliberate withholding of love. Carefully schooled 'not to let them see you cry,' I donned what must have appeared an extraordinarily heartless, callous mask of not caring. Inwardly I raged and grieved and mourned, writhing with guilt for ignoring Professor Witt's advice and letting myself be conned into aiding and abetting Geoffrey's destruction by the doubtless well-meaning but dotty treatment of the convivial pair at the officers' Convalescent Home. He was not the only patient to suffer either. There were men suffering permanent disabilities who would be completely well had they not been goaded into a hearty, hectic, outward bound, Duke-of-Edinburgh-Award-Winning-Scheme type campaign of convalescence. Had I fought, demanded a medical board, used my intelligence, the only, and improbable, risk might have been that of being left with a hypochondriac husband instead of a dead lover.

The call to say he had died – peacefully of course, has anyone ever heard from a hospital that a patient has died in gruelling agony? – came at six o'clock in the morning. I heard my mother answering the telephone and knew what it must be but I didn't get out of bed. I waited, numbly, for her to call me at eight o'clock with tea and sympathy. She had decided not to disturb me earlier and I was too cowardly to face facts before necessary; but then we had to get moving. My father had to be rung and told. I suggested leaving him to finish his holiday, accompanied by Lally and her friend Margot, while we coped with John's help, but the right thing had to be done, otherwise what would people say? He travelled down from Scotland overnight, walked straight past me as I sat in the kitchen and then plunged into a cold bath, followed by criticism of the railways for what, my mother was immediately to rectify, had been an inedible breakfast. "The whole business," he said, "was a confounded nuisance." And so it was. Geoffrey and I had never had a home of our own and here I was back to square one. There was one gainer though. My mother. By a whisker she had escaped losing me and now I was not only back, her sole property, but also back in a vulnerable state. She was needed again and – oh bliss – by me. I fell into the trap like a penny into a slot machine and out of the machine flowed an endless supply of goodies for her.

The treatment Geoffrey received at the hands of military doctors was so scandalous that, in spite of the fact that he had been demobilised, I received, on reporting the facts to my MP, Quintin Hogg, an officer's widow's full pension – usually awarded to those women whose husbands had been killed on active service.

After my brief fluttering from the nest she was in charge. Firstly, she decided I was not to be allowed to go to the funeral. I do not go to more funerals than duty dictates. The sick joke of the corpse having been 'our sister' or 'our brother' to half the congregation who may have been hitherto and are certainly forever now, unknown to them, or practically life-long enemy in-laws or hated spouses of business acquaintances, has ceased to amuse me. However, I do believe that it is possible that the sight of the coffin disappearing into the ground or sliding smoothly between those opulently swishing, cinema-style curtains may help the genuinely bereaved to face the fact that the occupant of the box will never be seen alive again, thus shortening the period during which they feel that, by some miracle, or even just wishful thinking, he will come back. For months I was confident that, if I were insistent enough, he would at any moment be there. I would catch tantalising glimpses of him in the street, see the back of his head four rows in front of me at the theatre, hear his husky "dearest, darling love, I do love you so much" as I fell asleep. I still have vivid dreams in which I can feel him, talk with him, even smell him. And all the next day he is near me, haunting me.

I was in my early twenties when he died and letters of sympathy poured in. One, from an elderly nun, Cecily Maude, a friend of my parents, emphasized my loss almost to hysteria – it was so frustrating that Geoffrey was not there to share the ineptitude of it with me. She wrote of the joy I must be experiencing in the knowledge that he was with God.

I cannot remember the exact words, but the gist of the message was that God would arrange an introduction between her long deceased mother and Geoffrey and what a consolation it must be to know they were together and that I eventually would be joining them. I imagined that ill-matched trio and, oddly, found the picture more comic than comforting.

In my desolation it seemed a long time to wait to discover whether God, my husband or I would find that three is not company and which of us would tactfully withdraw. I am not religious and believe reunions with the dead are, and ever will be, for me only in a fantasy world. If God is a father figure I've had as much as I can take of a father on earth and delightful though it would be to have faith in Him, heaven and all its perks, the God I occasionally and unsuccessfully appeal to in moments of extreme crisis is too punitive, too humourless, too devilishly oblivious of my needs for me to anticipate a pleasurable eternity hobnobbing with Him.

As for Geoffrey and me gallivanting about in white nightdresses, pantomime wings sprouting from our shoulders, playing 'our tune' on our harps; well...!

Secondly, thirdly and ad nauseam the goodies tumbling out

of the slot machine for my mother were an inexhaustible supply of "gastric flu", colds, sinus trouble and migraine after migraine. Anything in fact but ordinary, physical, curable illnesses. Back to the chaise longue I crawled, languidly reading, listening to music, not even wondering what, if anything, to do with the rest of my life sentence.

I half-heartedly tried and failed to get back into MI5.

Finally my mother was more anxious than fulfilled by my malaise and I had a short, disappointing career as a professional invalid. Disappointing because nervous exhaustion was diagnosed and I must rest. The problem was to devise ways of lengthening the days to include more rest than I was already having.

In much the same way, as a child, my vomiting was always attributed to rich gravy, chocolate, my being the only one in the family to have got the bit of fish that must have "gone off," cheese, bananas, or just my nerves. Just my nerves. What with the amazingly increasingly bizarre diets my mother, in collusion with successions of doctors too stupid to see the illness behind the symptoms – or, perhaps, wise enough to know when they had met their Waterloo – concocted for me, I must have had the constitution of a garbage disposal unit to survive at all.

The diagnosis that there was nothing physically wrong with me, as an adult, was a blow. There was no excuse for me to turn my face to the wall and wait to join Geoffrey, the nun's mother and God in heaven, the relentless game of life had to be played.

Very slowly recovering from my inertia there seemed no choice but to play at living, and I joined the first team of Merry Widows.

One of the parlour games attractive young widows have to learn is that of protecting themselves against *Matchmakers Inc.* Young widows are untidy and, worse, dangerous; still enticing enough for hosts to want them at parties, assumed to be on the prowl and in some Magistrates' Courts would, I imagine, along with swingeing fines, be the victims of pontificating matronly magistrates venomously denouncing them as menaces to society.

However young and attractive they are, *Matchmakers Inc.* ferrets out, sometimes with laudable intentions, bachelors, widowers and divorcées aged from twenty to seventy, with or without teeth, hair, paunches, intelligence or charm, and should you discourage the advances, if any, of these unattached but not for some reason quite as untidy as widows, men, M.I. is bewildered, astonished, hurt or downright angry, according to which saleswoman has fallen down on the job of pairing you off.

A minor discomfort, which I had to put up with now I was a widow, were the evenings when I was not out. My father always read aloud to my mother every single evening when he was at home. Directly after the evening meal the reading started. It lasted throughout the evening and went on after they were in bed. He read aloud to us children too, when we were young. It sounds a pleasant way to spend an evening but he chose the books and we had to concentrate because at any moment he would pounce on one of us and say: "What was the last word?" I endured it with fortitude but there were snags. It was boring to have to listen to a book I didn't enjoy and if I did enjoy the book, I would have preferred to read it, much faster, to myself. My mother said she had learnt the knack, in bed, of falling asleep lightly enough to wake up and repeat the last word on demand.

As an amusing social parasite I was so seldom at home in the evenings that when I was, I went to bed to catch up on sleep or read to myself. As a widow it was different. I went out often, but not as much as before. There was only one warm room in the house – the room where the readings were held. My taste in books was not my father's taste and even if it had been, great chunks would have been missed by me when I was out and during the bedtime story bits. There was absolutely nothing for me to do. I had to go to bed – in winter with two hot-water bottles, no fires in our bedrooms – and read. There was no radio for me. How fortunate that I am a compulsive reader, but I did sometimes wonder if they realised how lonely I was. I complained about it once. My father's solution was that I should stay in every night and listen; catching up with the chapters he had read in bed, the next day.

My father read aloud in a monotonous drone and I owe him a debt of gratitude for that too. I think I developed a talent for switching enough attention off to help me as an abridger. I do not inflict on the actors who read the serials for broadcasting with such talent and perception passages which, even if quite readable to oneself, are not ear-catching enough for the listeners.

※

After Geoffrey died, duty demanded that I should keep in touch with his parents – not only duty but a deep feeling of sympathy for them as one by one his contemporaries married, had children, and my in-laws were left without a family to gasp at and tut-tut over. I wrote regularly and often – they replied by return of post so I was always in debt. His parents had some friends, the Hipwells, who I thought, in my typically southern sentimental way, had an even drearier life than the rest of the inhabitants of Shipley, Yorkshire, the dark grey slate town in which they lived.

Mrs Hipwell had carelessly slipped onto a tramline when she was a child and had had her right hand neatly amputated by a tram. It was of no significance – she was fitted with increasingly larger china hands as she grew up and was able to bake, scrub and sew as did her friends. Once, when I said how awful it must be for her, I was very firmly squashed by my mother-in-law who viewed it with the precise amount of horror it merited, pointing out that her china hand was very good for making pastry, as it stayed cool for the purpose.

Not long after I had given way to that mawkish expression of my feelings, she wrote to tell me that the Hipwells had gone away for the weekend and on their way home, one of Mr Hipwell's legs felt cold. He must have created a stupid scene because on arrival at their house he had gone to bed and she had, with her china hand, filled a hot water bottle for him, but the next day his leg was so frozen that a doctor had to be called and within hours the leg was amputated.

I wasn't going to fall into the morbid trap of sympathy again so when I next wrote I added a postscript saying how sorry I was to hear of Mr Hipwell's misadventure, and hoped my postscript implied that six limbs between two people was a luxury with which any sensible couple should be able to cope perfectly happily.

Months passed before I heard any news of that lucky six-limbed pair again and then the latest bulletin was that his other leg had met the same chilly death. I thought that the news demanded a reply by return of post. A couple with only five out of the usual eight limbs between them did seem to me deserving of some notice even in the stoical North. On the contrary. Life was much easier for them. They had, naturally, bought a bungalow. He was a very keen gardener so he had a little wooden platform with wheels constructed for him and instead of all that kneeling first on one knee, then on the other, bending, stooping, crouching and finally giving up, he was tearing about on his platform all day every day tirelessly tending what was the showpiece garden of the neighbourhood.

Relieved of the burden of so many legs and hands, which make a misery of existence for most people, they were having the time of their lives. And a very long time it was too. They had not been young when I first met them but there is nothing like losing superfluous legs and hands for prolonging life. He died of old age.

My contacts with the North of England have made me very conscious of the soft lives we live in the South. Another friend of Geoffrey's parents spent seventeen years in hospital and was then discharged, miraculously cured. The morning he left hospital he went to revisit his club; the passage was dark, a trap door was open and he fell down it. Fortunately, not much damage was done. He was taken straight back to hospital but was discharged again in due course. My in-laws comment was that it would teach him to look where he was going in the future.

However, Yorkshire men have a healthily tender attitude towards 'brass.' First my mother-in-law and then my father-in-law died, and when I heard the news of his death, I was told by their solicitor that there was a complication in that my father-in-law had had a motor accident some months before which, unhappily, had been entirely his fault and could not be defended, and it had caused considerable damage to the other party. As sole beneficiary of what I knew to be an estate barely large enough to cover the simplest of funerals I had a frightening vision of supporting a widow with numerous children for the rest of my life.

"But surely," I said, "He was insured."

"Oh, yes, he was," the solicitor told me, "but only third party."

"In that case," I replied, "the insurance company will pay up, won't it?"

"Aye, it will," said the solicitor, "but the deceased will lose his no claims bonus."

∞

Two days after Geoffrey's death, my friend, Geneste, in Egypt, telegraphed an invitation to stay with them indefinitely, offering to pay my fare into the bargain. I had not the spirit to accept, but years later they moved to Holland and I went to stay with them there. They rang up the evening before I was due to leave England to warn me that the entire family had got mumps but I would still be welcome if prepared to risk infection. Off I went, to be received by four enormous, moon-faced smiles.

Mumps apart, it was a life-changing experience. Originally I planned to stay for about three weeks but they insisted that I extend my visit indefinitely and I was absorbed into a hitherto unknown world – that of a normal happy family. Geneste, married to Leslie Holliday, was the friend with whom I had learnt to make dinner tables into lily ponds, and to speed up our lives to keep pace with the jet set by writing 'Dear Sir' and 'Yours faithfully' in shorthand. She hated a pair of cherished old trousers Leslie had had before they were married. She begged, implored and finally insisted that he should throw them away. He refused. He liked them. One day, when he was out, she cut off one trouser leg at the knee. For the whole of the next weekend he wore them, without comment, with one whole and one half leg. He appeared to be oblivious of the comedy and Geneste and I were forced to spend two days giggling convulsively in her kitchen. She won, though, in the end, through me. She edged him carefully into a tiff about something quite different, and when he was really nettled, said: "PLEASE. I cannot allow this unpleasantness in front of our guest. It is too upsetting and embarrassing for her."

One way and another she taught me quite a few useful little tips on managing a family. One was the ability to present revolting food as treats. Never, she said, apologise for a failure. As you place a particularly repulsive dish on the table, you smile smugly and say: "Aren't you lucky today? I managed to find this delicious old family recipe, which you will all love. But please leave some over for tomorrow." You then subside wearily onto your chair. It works. They gobble it up.

They sometimes quarrelled, of course. The children were naughty and had to be disciplined, but discipline consisted of no meaning no, and yes meaning yes, or in extreme circumstances, deprivation of privilege. We adults spent hilarious evenings devising extravagant privileges for the children to be deprived of, if necessary.

After a few weeks, I decided I must work to pay my way. I applied for a job as a clerk at the British Embassy and was immediately accepted on condition that I supplied two references from England. I wrote to my father asking him to contact two friends of his – one was the Chairman of the Board of Inland Revenue who had advised my father not to let me attempt a ballet career – with titles and positions which would decorate the character references which I had been told by the Embassy were a mere formality. By return of post, I received the most inexplicable letter. It was from my father refusing to contact anyone. "It is gross chicanery to try to get yourself a job at the British Embassy. You are to come home immediately," he wrote. It was unbelievable! However, so indoctrinated was I with the assumption that anything my father said must be right that I abandoned the British Embassy, but I did not go home. I was having a glorious time again. Instead, I got a job, which in reality did involve me in chicanery. There was a little school in The Hague established, as its prospectus quaintly put it, for the children of ambassadors and their secretaries. There was a temporary vacancy on the staff; I applied for the post and got it.

My friends and I rehearsed the interview with the headmistress. I was to say that I came from Oxford. "What," Geneste asked, "if she asks you what you read there?" "Oh, *Gone With the Wind*," I said. Luckily the question was not asked and, irresponsibly, I undertook the teaching of reading, writing and arithmetic to twenty four-and-five year old children of different nationalities. I was useless.

Charles Robert Tuthill Hickson at The Hague c. 1949.

Janet Mary on engagement to Charles Hickson.

Newlyweds: Charles and Janet at The Hague.

Charles and Janet's honeymoon.

Janet, Charles and Robert.

Janet, Charles and Robert.

Robert Hickson as a toddler.

Robert Hickson as a toddler.

John Veale.

Janet Hickson, *née* Veale.

It was at one of Geneste's house parties that I met Charles Hickson. Charles was Irish, charming, witty and, clever. I discovered he had an unusual streak, which was the opposite of the ex-public school, slightly cold-centred young men with whom I had had relationships, which would have passed muster with my mother. He was a geologist with Shell, temporarily off fieldwork owing to a gastric ulcer diagnosed in Trinidad. He drove a vast Ford Essex car, which attracted much amusement in The Hague, along with requests to photograph it for publication in the Dutch press. It was our transport to Brussels for numerous weekend visits. Once, during a week of evenings out, Geneste mentioned that her neighbours were curious about what we were up to in the Essex outside their flat in The Hague almost every night until three or four o'clock in the morning.

This was not love at first sight as had so often been the case with boyfriends in Oxford – and which had as quickly led to disillusionment. It was a friendship, which grew stronger and deeper with every meeting until it developed into the amazing bondage of love.

༼༽

Charles and I were married on a cold day in February. Charles not having been warned about my unsatisfactory character by my father. All went well, including a brief reception in the Corpus Dining Hall – brief because my father was footing the bill. We had a romantic honeymoon driving down to Cannes where, oddly for Cannes, it was snowing hard. Stopping off in Brussels, after our honeymoon, we booked into a hotel for the night. We left our luggage, which included suitcases given to me as wedding presents and packed with my hard-earned expensive trousseau, in the car. On returning in the morning, we found it had been broken into and all my luggage stolen. I've never since that morning felt the same affection for Brussels.

Unlike some girls, I did not subconsciously seek a father-like mate. Quite the reverse. Charles was a born looker-after-er and I think he was as near to being a male heterosexual mother-figure, without my mother's insatiable needs, as it would be possible to find. We were very happy at the beginning of our marriage in a little flat in Scheveningen, but within four months, I was pregnant and the looking-after began in earnest. Patiently he coped with morning, afternoon, evening and night sickness. He shopped, cleaned and cooked while I, reclining, repressed irrational, hysterical fears. I felt simply terrible for three months and then made a partial recovery when visiting my mother in England, but was it the usual post-first-three-months of pregnancy turn for the better? I was more ill than ever when I went back to Holland.

A month or so later, Charles was told he was to be posted to Borneo and he decided that he could not face the rigours of a geologist's life in the field and resigned his job. We had nowhere to go so went home to Oxford for an indefinite period. And there we stayed for two years.

On March 6th, we went to the New Theatre to see T.S. Eliot's play, *The Cocktail Party*. I had had pains during the day and after the play I went to the loo and the waters broke. My ignorance about childbirth was total. I told my mother what had occurred and she instructed Chas to take me to the Radcliffe Infirmary, where the baby was to be born. I was having very painful contractions. I was left completely alone, crying and moaning until eventually the night sister poked her head round the door, denied that I was having pains and ordered me to be quiet as the mother next door, whose baby was dead inside her, found it disturbing. Soon after that Professor Chasser Moir, who was my obstetrician (as a member of the Faculty of Medicine, he had dealings with my father and was also in charge of Lally's pregnancy) came to see me and immediately sent a nurse to stay with me and very soon after that I lost consciousness and the baby was born. Chas was, of course, sent home before any of this drama. Robert, our son, was what was described to me as a 'funny colour' and was sent into exile in an oxygen tent on another floor. Sister glanced at me, asking what he was to be called in case he died before being christened. For the next four days I was milked by machine for a baby we had not seen. However, some time during that four days, the day sister, Sister Grey, who was as gentle and kind as the night sister was sadistic, took us down to see Robert in his oxygen tent. When he was well enough to come to me to be fed, I would crouch over him when he had finished, telling him over and over again that I promised that I would 'make it up' to him. I meant to compensate him for having inflicted life on him; life which I didn't see as such a blessing.

I ought to have been content. My mother was a good cook and willing baby-sitter. Robert was a textbook infant and I overflowed with milk for him. He fed and slept and gurgled and grinned his gorgeous gummy, adoring grin at me and yet I had weeks of post-natal depression during which I would wake up at three o'clock in the morning, shaking, desperate and panic-stricken. When I was with Robert, I loved him but the thought of him terrified me. From three o'clock in the morning until seven when I fed him, I lay awake and worked out how long it would be before he could go to school. Supposing he went when he was seven and I managed to struggle through those seven years, how would I cope with the holidays? I prayed frantic prayers that I would die, that I would wake up to find the mess was a nightmare to be forgotten.

Charles joined ICI and went into dreary digs, coming down to us at weekends. He searched London for a flat or house and each one he found had to be inspected by my mother and each was out of the question. There were too many stairs for me and a pram. The bedroom was too small. The kitchen was dirty. They were like my suitors of the old days. They had to be impeccable and none of them was. Eventually, he found a plot in Surrey on which to build a house.

We drove down to look at our 'plot' that we had bought to build on, and my spirits sank lower and lower as we delved further and further into lush, rich, ordered Surrey. As my spirits sank, so my guilt increased. I was not excited at the prospect of an architect-designed house of my own. In fact, I was sick with apprehension. When we arrived at the plot, houseless, empty, a sloping field surrounding one old baked bean tin and one old car tyre, my spirits rose. It would take ages before a house grew there and, in the meantime, it should not be difficult to play the role of frustrated wife and mother, living at home as I always thought of it, separated from Monday to Friday from Charles, and bewail the fact. I quickly grew into the part and, between daunting visits to the reality of the house being built, I did look forward in rare moments of uncharacteristic optimism to living the life of a normal woman with a baby.

Robert was two by the time the house was ready and we had

arranged for an au pair girl, one of many to follow, to act as my first line of defence between total responsibility and family life. Having made the move, I was temporarily absorbed in housework. I loved the house, and put all my energies into keeping it sparklingly polished and tidy. Unlike most au pair girls, mine always had Saturdays and Sundays free so that Chas was available to protect me from responsibility for Robert. And one girl punctually arrived a week before another left at the end of her year, so that there was never a gap for me to weather on my own.

When Charles had to go away on business the rest of us went to stay in Oxford. Gradually the visits became longer and longer and were not confined to periods of grass widowhood.

I used to hear myself saying things to Robert which had been said to me by my parents, things that jarred on me. I felt uncomfortable with myself. Many incidents stand out in my mind. Once, when he was being particularly maddening I said: "There are special schools for naughty boys like you and if you don't behave I shall send you to one." I made that threat to a three year old. Another time the devil was really working for me. My son was frightened of thunder. He was irritating me and I said: "If you go on like this it may thunder," at which moment a thunderclap crashed directly over the roof. I was astounded and nearly as frightened as he was.

I did not, however, use my mother's most effective weapon. Faced with the slightest deviation from the behaviour she demanded of me, she would announce that if I didn't do as she wanted, she would have to tell my father and *he* would be cross with *her*.

Later, with insight, I patiently and concentratedly undid the harm I had done him. We enforced discipline to make him feel safe with himself. I learnt to show that I was human and could be cross too, but he was never threatened with anything more disastrous than missing children's television – and miss it he did, over and over again, but in an atmosphere of acceptance. The deprivation of television over, all was forgotten.

Before that time, he was the victim of the confusion I lived in. We all were. I lost all interest in the house. I rejected Charles more and more as a husband and leant more and more heavily on him as a mother-nurse figure. I felt increasingly isolated, and stealthily, one by one, my old neuroses crept up on me. I was never well. I had the familiar sensation of being on the outside looking in. I did not belong. I was not a normal married woman with a good husband, a little boy and a charming house however much I told myself I was. I counted my blessings and sank deeper and deeper into depression. I considered suffering humanity and could not identify with it. I was suffering more acutely. There were no burdens to crush me and I knew it. I was guilty of nothing, but my guilt swamped me.

I spent more and more time in bed, or silently gliding from one piece of furniture to another, wringing my hands, clutching at shelves, tables and chairs and the words, "Oh, woman, woman" sobbed in my head, occasionally escaping from my lips as a whisper – a whisper – an almost inaudible whisper, when I was alone in the house. I gazed at myself in the mirror for reassurance. Reassurance about what? That I existed? Did I want to exist? Hoping that the mirror would reflect the nothing that I felt myself to be? I gazed out of windows as prisoners gaze between the bars of their cells.

Nothing happened. There was no relief. Nothing interested me. I could no longer read. I ran the house like an automaton. People said I looked thin and even how lucky I was to be so slim – I was terribly underweight – but no one noticed that I was really ill. I was not withdrawn to the extent that my social sense failed me when I needed it and I could exchange pleasantries with neighbours, shop assistants and my 'au pair' girls without them knowing that, under the bright surface, was a chasm at the bottom of which my real self barely existed.

Everything became routine, nothing was new. I got up and went to bed, and between getting up and going to bed I went to bed in the daytime. I wanted nothing. I not only lacked zest for life, I would have preferred to die; but not positively enough. I gazed at bottles of sleeping tablets, the gas stove, the drop from the balcony to the terrace outside the house and all action seemed too much trouble. I offered myself imaginary treats. Trips round the world. Countless millions of pounds. And on all the treats I turned my back. I wanted nothing. There was nothing I wanted. I wanted nothing. I WAS nothing. For the last time in my life I went home to my mother.

For a little while, with her aid, my distress was thinly

masked beneath so many seemingly physical symptoms that it would have been a very irresponsible doctor who would have failed to set me on a long course of physical examinations. They went through me with a toothcomb and on each test I had I pinned my hopes. Each one would prove that I had a grumbling – shouting – appendix, an ulcer, was anaemic, even had a brain tumour – a tumour anywhere, something physical, anything, anything at all which could be treated with pills, operated on, even amputated and the result would be the end of my symptoms and would usher in a new era of well-being, normality, a new me, a happy me, a person like other people, a loving wife, brave mother, competent, confident and adequate. It would end the blackest depression, the longest depression, the most irrational depression that anyone had ever known.

Every time the toothcomb failed to find even the tiniest organic disorder, I was hurled miles down the bottomless pit, the fathomless depths of despair. The world itself seemed too small to contain my suffering. After each examination, as I doubtingly awaited the news that I had something that could be put right, I became more despairing. My hopes turned tail and became more and more set on the solution of inoperable tumours and untreatable, intractable, galloping fatal diseases. Beaming doctors would bound into my room with the unwelcome good news that all was well; and at each beaming doctor I glowered, greeting the news with helpless despairing tears. Merrily they went their ways, unaware of the catastrophes they had comforted me with.

Another difficulty was the inquisitions to which I had to submit. Doctors represented authority. However patiently, gently and quietly they questioned me – and they were not all patient, gentle and quiet – the consultations were disastrous and traumatic. I tried to be co-operative but so many questions could not be answered with a plain "yes" or "no" and before each inquisition I felt guilty. I felt that they would assume I was lying – indeed I felt that I would be lying and I know now that that was a hangover from the torturing inquisitions of us by my father.

As a child, if I was alone in the garden and he watched me tread on forbidden ground – a just-that-minute hoed flowerbed, for instance, he would not pounce, accuse and punish. He would question. Whose footmark was that? Who had been in the garden with me? Who had trodden on the flowerbed? Did I realise that it was wrong to tread on flowerbeds? What did I think the punishment for treading on a flowerbed would be? And so on. And so on. And when the final question came – had *I* trodden on the flowerbed? – The truthful answer might have been, "well yes and no." Yes in the sense that it was my footmark, but no in the sense that I had not deliberately trodden there. I had slipped, had not noticed, couldn't remember. It was too difficult for me to reply to the questions truthfully because I just did not know the answers.

The same with the doctors. I could not describe symptoms. If I said they were acute, I immediately felt I was exaggerating.

When I said they were tolerable, at the moment of saying so, I remembered being stabbed, incapacitated by them. They were up against a contradictory patient. Sometimes I could feel their irritation and felt they hated me, thought I was wasting their time, wished I was a straightforward 'case' with which they could cope and I guessed what I thought they would like me to say and aimed to please by saying it.

Here again I was reminded of my father's inquisitions when I was a child concerning what I was reading. As I have said, there was no censorship, but there was enough fuss to put anyone off books for life. To begin with, I always had my nose in a book instead of being out in the fresh air – but if I wanted to read at all – and I was an addict – there wasn't an endless amount of time available for inhaling fresh air because, once started, a book had to be finished. Ploughing your way through *Sir Walter Scott* at the age of seven is hard work and a book had to be finished in a week and there could be no cheating because of the tests. Skipping was almost as bad as lying. Not understanding was the inevitable result of my notorious lack of application – a very serious fault and most infuriating of all were the spot checks on the precise whereabouts of books which had to be replaced in the right space on a bookshelf for a certain length of time before being allowed out again.

There was to be no easy way out for me. I had to have a nervous breakdown. I was obsessed by worry after worry and fear after fear. I was afraid of being alone. I was afraid of people. I was afraid of going out and I had claustrophobia indoors. I knew I was going mad. I was afraid I was changing my sex. I was in a long, dark red, blood red tunnel and a tunnel without end. I had fantasies of weird operations being performed on me by wickedly masked doctors and nurses cackling with mirth as they stuck shining, steel needles into my stomach and head.

Two of my fantasies were beautiful. One was that if I could escape from knowing what I knew I would find that I was, in reality, an elegant, silky, purring, cosseted, amber-eyed black cat. The other was the most joyful, free, lovely picture imaginable. It may not even have been a fantasy at all. There is, by the river in Oxford, a large green area called Port Meadow, which by some ancient right provides free grazing for horses. Occasionally, it is said, the horses gallop out of the meadow – and that is what may actually have happened. It was a brilliant moonlit night in the middle of which I heard galloping horses – hooves. I got up and there, streaming down Banbury Road, between No 29, our house, and the entrance to the University Parks, came horses, singly, in couples and in groups. Black, chestnut, grey, white they passed beneath my window, manes and tails flowing and gleaming in the light of the full moon. I watched and watched, fascinated and each time I thought the last horse had galloped by, there would be the sound of more of those gloriously undisciplined horses having their moonlit spree.

I shall never forget it. The beauty of it was so intense and the intensity of it was intensified for me by the symbolism of spontaneous gaiety, breaking away, mischief, and uninhibited fun.

I was certain I would land up with a psychiatrist and that was one of the worst fears of all. Psychiatrists knew all about you. I imagined they pointed to your guilt and made you feel like a criminal. Worse, I had been warned, they made you dependent on them. The horror of that, of being dependent on another person filled many sleepless nights with anguish. I was afraid of being dependent when I had made a profession of dependency! The most appalling of all the appalling things I was cringing from was the possibility that I might be neurotic. Neurotic is still a fairly dirty word – how often is it said of someone: "Oh, he/she is impossible. So neurotic." Sometimes a diagnosis by someone so blissfully unaware of their own neuroses that, in self-defiance, they have to project their lack of self-awareness onto another person as a failing.

Other people seemed as grey, as depersonalised, and as negative as I felt. I could no longer face anything and lay in bed having nightmarish daydreams or nightmarish nightmares. I withdrew completely from my family. I ate nothing at all.

My mother's pitiful imploring of me to eat just a little, just to please her, sounded like gibberish. No one understood what was going on, least of all myself. My mother started complaining that she was too old to look after us all and that my father, who ignored me, was annoyed with her because I did not pull myself together. I did not care. Charles's weekend visits neither increased nor diminished my depression. He brought me presents. He offered me treats – visits to theatres, cinemas, new clothes. It was like offering a grain of sand to a homeless family to build a house on. All my senses were affected and, during that time – days? weeks? months? – I think I actually saw from my window a dull, lustreless, grey rose in full bloom, adorning a grey bush in a grey garden.

At that time I had one friend whom I trusted. He was a very overworked, very enlightened, very patient GP. Having run upstairs, he would sit as though I were his only patient, his only interest in life, and listen to me, at first almost without comment but finally, tactfully, gently, unobtrusively and sympathetically, planting a seed here, an idea there, a glimpse of somewhere else that suggested that my antipathy towards psychiatry was misplaced. Diplomatically, he agreed that not all psychiatrists were helpful – more diplomatically he persuaded me that, anyway, just one visit to one could do no harm. After the doctor's almost daily visits he would leap down the stairs and out of the house as though it were on fire, to sit, as my mother observed, writing notes before driving away.

My brother backed him up. He too, patiently and at great length, reassured me. He told me I was terribly neurotic and assured me that terribly neurotic was not a terrible thing to be. Except, of course, for the terribly neurotic sufferer.

There was a cult film at the time which John and I had seen. It depicted a lunatic asylum and was entitled *The Snake Pit*. John warned me that the Maudsley Hospital in London, where I was to have my consultation, was exactly like it with writhing snakes and a cast of screaming lunatics. John, in his own way, could be destructive.

∞

After much wasted time, I agreed to see a psychiatrist. Craftily, my most patient of all doctors, Dr Gillet, called very early on the morning Charles was to drive me up to London for what I assumed would be a crash course cure, lasting possibly half an hour, of all my ills. Breezily, Dr Gillet wished me good luck and, in an aside, airily suggested that it might be as well to pack a small suitcase.

"A suitcase?" I asked, then as suspicion became panic, "a suitcase – whatever for? They won't keep me there, will they?"

He was an honest man and he was in a predicament. He knew that if he said I might be kept in I would, most likely, refuse to go.

"Well, you know what hospitals are," he said cheerfully, calmly. "There might be a mistake in the time of your appointment so that you would have to stay the night in London or they might want you in for a night or so for blood tests or something."

I had waited many hours in many departments of hospitals for tests of every imaginable kind. I knew with what meticulous care patients were given exact times for their appointments with strict instructions not to be late, and how very rarely these times coincide with any activity on the part of the medical staff. I promised him that I would not only go, but that I would go with luggage.

John told me afterwards that during the evening of my admission to hospital, he called on my parents. I think he did so more in the zealous, missionary spirit of the enlightened out to enlighten than to offer them any comfort. He was furiously angry with them, in fact, for having damaged me so brutally. A display of furious anger is not the best form of propaganda to use when offering the blind their sight so he did his best, he reported later, by explaining with restrained civility that at last I was getting a chance to be well and that it was the only sort of treatment which could possibly help. My father simply went to his study to get on with his work. My mother, white-faced, turned on my brother. For once in her life she was more angry than hurt – but she was hurt too.

"How could you? How could you?" she kept repeating, and then, "after all I've done for her. Just when I had got her so much better. Just when everything was all right." I had barely got out of bed for weeks. She had bewailed the fact that it was all too much for her. "This time I really can't forgive you."

That evening it sent her rushing out of the room. Back to her bed.

༄

I went to the Maudsley Hospital. I was initially interviewed by the top man himself, Professor Sir Aubrey Lewis, who seemed to me ferocious beyond description. During the drive up to London my depression was split for a second or two by a fleeting moment of optimism, optimism that the great doctor would mysteriously make me better. But the optimism was suffocated almost before it was born by the feeling that my reality was real, forever, and that nothing could be done for me. "You are hopelessly neurotic and wicked," he would say, and I would be incarcerated for the rest of my life in a padded cell. A padded cell, though, for what reason? I did not want to express anything, hit out, damage people or objects.

We arrived so early for my appointment that we stopped for coffee before going on to the hospital. Sitting at the Formica table in a café, I could hardly believe in the situation. Seeking some kind of comfort I put my hand out to Charles.

"What's that for?" he said, and removed it to my lap. It was at that moment that I knew that there was no hope for me. No one would ever understand. After all the anguish of facing insanity, of changing my sex, of nameless, formless, literally indescribable panics and despair, I had reached the bottom and knew it; and in a curious, dark, hopeless way, I was resigned. I had no feelings.

I was not, as it turned out, acutely ill. I was put straight into the convalescent ward with all its privileges of unlocked doors, freedom to go out into London to hairdressers or meet friends, and freedom to have visitors. Heaven knows what the patients who had worked their way up to the convalescent ward must have suffered. I was warned by the "ferocious" Professor Sir

Aubrey, who advised me to register as an in-patient, that I might not find the company on the ward entirely congenial. They were mostly East-Enders and perhaps he thought that, with my background, it would be difficult for me to make friends. I think they viewed me, initially, with slight suspicion and they teased me about my la-di-dah ways but they were warm-hearted, and we all found that not only were we in the same boat but we were just the sort of people with whom we would have chosen to share our boat. The hospital was typical of its kind. Hardly room to fit a locker between each bed, nowhere to hang any clothes, no laundry facilities, and an all-pervading smell of lavatories. I was all right because Charles could take my washing away to be dealt with at home – wherever home was. However, the nurses were kind and after my first night when I was overpowered by the terror of knowing that I had allowed myself to become in my estimation not a certified, but at any rate an official lunatic, the change of environment worked well. I wanted to make a good impression. I scrubbed the acres of brown linoleum in the ward to show the other patients that la-di-dah I might be, but I was not above taking on my share of ward chores. The food was marvellous, and in six weeks I swelled from six to eight stone. We had fun. We laughed. There were socials and dances in the evenings and I, naturally, was drawn to a man who danced like a professional. We were relieved of all home ties and responsibilities.

Having again been the focus of my mother's special catering and nursing skills, I had lost so much weight that on arrival at the Maudsley, I was put on a special diet. From under seven stone, I emerged six weeks later having gained a stone and have remained around eight stone ever since.

However, not all the patients had the comparatively easy time I had. Some of them regressed and had to be moved back to other wards. Groups, with ever-available sympathy, would form round a weeping woman. People had sudden panics and were unable to go down to the canteen for meals. Always the stories of suffering ran on. Early environments made mine seem like some enchantingly beautiful fairy tale. Appalling recent tragedies. One woman had seen her two children run over and killed. One was the sole survivor of a whole family burnt to death in a fire. Frequently the catastrophe with which someone was learning to cope was obvious – she was the 'well' one with a husband so sick, but unaware of the fact, that it might have been more profitable for him to be having psychiatric treatment while leaving her in peace in the outside world.

There was only one nurse I did not like. She was determined to find out everything about us all. She was not unkind, but her prying questions irritated all the patients. When my turn came for the probing I told her I had eleven sons in eleven years and that I only liked one of them. I did some quick thinking up of eleven boys' names and she never bothered me again. She did not know whether or not I was teasing her, but I refused to change my story for her. The smallness of the world seemed smaller there when a girl alcoholic appeared in the ward. She was a talented artist and we became very friendly. The only thing I really hated was Occupational Therapy. I have never been able to sew and the sight of wickerwork makes me shudder. In fact, I discovered in hospital that there is nothing I can do with my hands, but I had to go to Occupational Therapy and so they found me a typewriter and I practiced 'The quick brown fox jumps over the lazy dog' over and over again! It didn't seem to help my typing much but it passed the time.

One odd fact – though I was truly fond of my friends in hospital, once out of it I never wanted, under any circumstances, to see any of them again.

While I was there, I forgot my family and they, apparently, forgot me. Not unexpectedly, during my incarceration I never heard from my parents. My mother turned her back on the whole unpleasant incident and, Charles told me, studiously avoided any reference to it. I never heard from my father. A few months before I broke down, I had a sinus operation in the nursing home literally next door but one from his house. I was in the home for ten days and my father neither visited nor enquired about me.

I constantly asked if he knew I was there. Of course – he disregarded all illnesses. Titled friends were given a very cold shoulder if idiotic enough to succumb to cancer or heart attacks. Charles was amazed by my father's lack of concern about me. My mother said:

"Well, you know what he is. Very busy at the Registry."

Years after, the unspeakable stigma, the deplorable lack of

'moral fibre' which had transformed me into a daughter of whom the less said the better, I had a hysterectomy. It was entirely, wholesomely physical and my mother, joyfully, was not only able to suffer more than I did, but could not talk about it to everyone, rake in sympathy for herself and even send me a bed jacket to cheer me up. My father never mentioned the episode, did not enquire about me and was, I think, my only acquaintance not even to send me a 'Get Well' card. I got one from my hairdresser. I refused to believe John who said, "Well, of course, it's in his interest that you should recover." After the agony of the post-operation two or three days had worn off, I had the holiday of a lifetime sunbathing on the roof of Guys Hospital, getting up a tan and complaining, as did the other patients, that our sundeck lacked only white-coated stewards whizzing about among our visitors with trays of drinks.

In the "bin" the only times I cried were when I was asked – no forcing there – to describe my childhood and family. Gently and sympathetically my doctor, Brian Davis, drew my attention to the frequent, slanted, unconscious displays of resentment I showed towards my mother. My feelings towards my father had always been so overtly, healthily hostile that it was only by noting my compulsive self-denigration that they had to be looked into at all. After six weeks, fattened up for the slaughter of psychotherapy, I collected up my understandably grumpy son and 'au pair' girl, to go back to Surrey and attend the Maudsley Hospital as an outpatient.

I had had a nervous breakdown. I had had friends who had had nervous breakdowns. As far as I was concerned, it was much the same as measles. You were ill, you recovered, people were mildly sympathetic, asked once or twice how you were and that was that. I was wrong.

The mother of a child with whom I had formerly taken turns in driving our children to school rang up and, without reason, said she thought it better if she took her child to school herself in future. Another acquaintance, not a friend, telephoned on the slimmest of pretexts, referred to my stay in hospital and put me through an inquisition: Was it like *The Snake Pit*? What had the other "loonies" been like? Had I been in a straight jacket? The local clergy converged on me separately and en masse like scavenging seagulls wailing their forlorn cries behind fishing boats. I was obviously ripe for conversion. One called and said he knew all about me. He had married a psychiatrist himself, he told us, and knew that all psychiatrists were mad themselves and that if I ever felt like hacking Robert, who was in the room at the time, to death with a hatchet, he suggested that I contact him first. As it happened, my au pair girl of the moment, an Austrian, had had a breakdown herself, after a car crash in which she had seen her fiancé killed, and winked a comforting wink at me.

Another clergyman asked to see the house and when we got to the bedroom, groped me.

Psychotherapy is said to be a long, slow, painful process. For me it was to relive the horrors of childhood, face and reject the distorted pictures of devoted, self-sacrificing parents which had been imprinted on my mind and to reject, revise and accept them, to see them as the damaging, destructive dervishes they were and emerge reborn and find my own identity. It is a steep and slippery climb with many hidden rocks on which to become impaled. But I did it – or, rather, we did it. My doctors listened, and listened with warmth, shrewdness and empathy. Accepting, absorbing and slowly pointing the way to new attitudes, new slants and always patiently, gently, reassuringly accepting resentment, spite, anger and the other sides of all the coins – humour, good manners and love. They were always there for appointments, never condemning, sometimes demolishing in order to reconstruct and, at the very last, presenting me with freedom to FEEL. When I broke down, I was told that my best hope of recovery was to be true to myself. I, misunderstanding what was meant, took it so much to heart that before saying, "good morning," to the milkman, I used to take several seconds for serious assessment as to whether it really was a good morning, and whether I thought so.

∽∽

There is one disadvantage in undergoing psychotherapy at a teaching hospital. That is the inevitable changes of doctors. Part of the treatment for me consisted of learning to form a trustful relationship in which I could reveal myself. My first doctor was a man, Dr Major Eilenberg. It was a long time before I felt safe enough with him to describe even the depths of my depressions. During my time with him, I once had a terrible fantasy of killing Robert. I was so frightened that I went up to London and spent the day at Waterloo station until it was time to meet Geneste to see Michael Flanders and Donald Swann at the Foretune Theatre. The next day, I went to see my GP, Dr Dockrey. When he asked me what the matter was, I could only say, "I am frightened of losing my temper." His waiting room was full and it was such a silly illness to take to him that he hardly listened to me before terminating the consultation. When I got home and saw Robert, I, myself, could not believe that I had wasted a day at Waterloo station to save his life. When I next saw Dr Eilenberg, I told him every detail of that day. With him it was safe to re-experience the gruesome details I had imagined of meeting my son when he was brought home from nursery school and bashing his head on the terrace over and over again, until the blood spurted over the paving stones and he was dead, dead, dead. I was reliving my childhood fantasy of killing my brother. Dr Eilenberg listened in silence and when I finished he said: "Yes?" Tears poured down my cheeks. "Why do you cry?" he asked. I cried because of the relief of telling him and with astonishment that he reacted so calmly, so causally and yet so warmly, as if I had told him of the breaking of a saucer. I had been afraid he would call the police. I wanted to be reassured that I would never, in fact, lose control. His very lack of earnest reassurance was enough. "No," he told me, "you will never damage anyone but yourself – and that is only in your mind." He said it almost disdainfully – as though the episode was so ordinary, so dull, medically speaking, that an outburst about the weather would have been more dramatic. And I have never since had the slightest fear of losing control. I lose my temper often. I speak sharply and sometimes regret it. But hurt, kill? No.

Fairly soon after that session my doctor was moved to another hospital and I was posted, as it were, to a woman therapist. All my instincts told me that a woman was not to be trusted. She would fail me. She would be thinking about clothes while pretending to listen to me. She would vaguely and charmingly miss appointments, be late, indiscreet, abandon me, be unreliable in every way. Dr Eilenberg thought it probable that a woman doctor was exactly what I needed. He was, at that time, right, but I could not believe it. I made up my mind. If a woman was all they could offer me, I would be as unco-operative as possible. I would tell her nothing. I would be the one to be late. I would miss appointments. I would not only hate her, but I would tell her I hated her. That would demolish her and she would be replaced by a man. Her name was Dr Vivienne Cohen.

I went along trembling but trying to look snooty for my first appointment with that frivolous, unreliable, dreary, silly woman doctor and was instantly and completely disarmed. She was young, she was attractive and she had the widest, warmest smile – grin – imaginable. I felt encircled in warmth. I told her how much I had dreaded seeing her and how much I was going to hate her and, instead of rushing wounded and deeply offended out of the room, she looked straight into my eyes and said, "Yes, I know. Tell me. Tell me more." She was startlingly clever and, to my astonishment, whenever I was cross she appeared to lean closer, to care more, to welcome my hostility and, most surprisingly of all, still be there for our next session. She was truthful, honest and wise.

After a few sessions with her, just as I was becoming more sure of her, more secure, she went on holiday. She warned me that she had bad news for me and then told me that she would be away for ten days. My immediate reaction was despair. She would, I felt, never come back. Again, I was to be abandoned, helpless, uncared for. She said very empathetically "but you will be my very first patient on the very first day I come back." Momentarily I was comforted, but those ten days were the longest, darkest, dreariest slogs of the many slogs I have known. My whole life seemed as though it would forever be dingy and yet, like a crack splitting its way jaggedly along an icy pond, a refrain ran through my head constantly. It did not cheer me at the time, but remembering it now it seems as though, during my black despair, it was a thread, a hair's breadth of hope, a lifeline. For no reason, as I ploughed my way through that interminable ten days it murmured insistently, imploring for attention. It was "Oh brave new world, that has such people in it."

She taught me all I know about bringing up children, and whenever I was faced with a problem with Robert I had her persona at my disposal and could use it at home. I found that, as far as he was concerned, 'being' her was nearer to 'being' me than I had ever been as a mother when things I had said to him had jarred on my sensibilities. I discovered that I could not accept the short-term peace of false promises, threats to "tell Daddy" and that truth and an un-devious discipline worked better for us both. Gradually the antagonism with which he had naturally and healthily met me when I came out of the hospital changed to trust and companionship. Charles was an ideal father, very affectionate, with an endless supply of what my son found hilarious jokes.

From the practical point of view he was almost too good a father. Tremendously skilful with his hands, so whatever the damage, Robert would say, complacently looking at a cup in smithereens, thrown in a rage on the floor, or a clockwork toy broken beyond repair, "It's all right. When Daddy comes home he will mend it," and miraculously Daddy did seem able to mend almost anything.

He was not, however, quite so adept at helping to mend me. He was much too good for me, much too patient and yet unable to show his emotions. Of course, he'd had a basinful of emotions flying in all directions from me and was very much afraid of hurting me. I was well enough, desensitised enough, though, to take the rough and tumble (particularly the tumble) of married life and he had got stuck in the role in which he excelled – that of a protector. Dr Cohen encouraged the preservation of that status quo.

When everything has broken down in your life it would clearly be highly hazardous to demolish the last shaky foundations of family life. Where there is a child to consider it would be risky and Dr Cohen helped me build on myself, my true image of myself as a good mother. She concentrated on me and she was always ready to help me disentangle the sensible, warm, sometimes angry mother I really was from the smothering, suffocating never cross type I had known and was in danger of mimicking. My marriage was somehow slithered over, bypassed, evaded – and I was a very willing accomplice. She helped me climb out of depressions and she managed to bend the rules so that I stayed with her in the different departments of the hospital to which she was assigned. Somehow, she always found time to see me and even manipulated my visits away from the Maudsley to Guy's when the time came for her promotion. My sessions dwindled from one a week to one every two or three months and those meetings became more or less social occasions.

My only criticism of her treatment was that my marital difficulties were so minimised by her that I did not face them head-on myself. Doctors have their own moral and personal codes and ethics, and in that one respect I think perhaps she failed. It must have seemed so unlikely that any price would have to be paid that she was risking very little, but when Robert was in his teens I think that it was my turn to have a chance of being unlabelled. I had been my mother's *yes-girl*, Charles' fragile, sensitive, dependent (again) wife and my son's mother, but I had still to have a stab at just being me.

My parents, on visits to us, never hesitated to skate on very thin ice with me, continually referring to weak-minded acquaintances having nervous breakdowns, retreating into mental homes, "giving way" to silly illnesses. The patients were mostly working class, thus letting down their employers. I was tempted to say, "You are in my house making derogatory remarks about people who, as you well know, are suffering as I have suffered. You have a right to despise them but you have no right to trample on my sensibilities," but I was unwilling to hurt their feelings. On one of their visits, knowing my views on the subject, my mother could not resist the opportunity of stirring up a little war in my peaceful drawing room. "Was it not shocking" she asked me "that according to the press a boys' public school was going to take a limited number of girls into the sixth form?" In what I knew and intended would encourage the hostilities she wanted, I agreed with her – adding that it seemed such a pity to limit the number and to the sixth form at that.

She had blown the starting whistle and we were off. My father not only knew what was best for the pupils, but furthermore knew what students needed and wanted and in this instance what was best, what was needed, and what was wanted coincided – and not only at schools. A survey in which he had been involved, carried out when he was an undergraduate, had shown that the overwhelming majority of undergraduates (male) did not want any opening of doors to females. I had to take his word for the peculiar attitudes of his generation of undergraduates but as far as co-educational schools went, I had something to say. What I had to say was not even just my own contemptible opinion. I had heard a discussion on the radio the day before on the subject of letting girls seep into boys' schools and I was in a position to tell him that a most distinguished and well-known psychiatrist, Dr Miller, had been entirely in favour of co-education and had said words to the effect that tender relationships between adolescents at school, far from hindering their academic progress, appeared to have a beneficial emotional effect on both sexes, and on their scholastic performance.

"Ah," said my father, "that's where you're wrong. You don't realise that the psychiatrists only see abnormal people and are therefore the least qualified to judge." Added to which he knew the psychiatrist I was quoting to be a notorious charlatan in the medical world. "Ah-ha," said I, "then you are assuming that psychiatrists do not meet normal people, even outside working hours. They don't have normal friends. They are the offspring of schizophrenics (in parenthesis, humans, so far as my father was concerned, were either 'normal' or 'schizophrenic') so his distinguished colleagues in the psychiatric world are in clover as far as diagnosing is concerned, live their social lives among the abnormal, marry abnormal spouses and produce abnormal children."

I was, as usual, making wild generalisations, exaggerating, and talking about things I knew nothing about. I had no right to have any opinion on the subject. What he had meant was that all their adolescent patients were abnormal which was what made the doctors the worst possible judges of what was best in educational matters, and were, into the bargain and for the same reason, totally unfit to deal with the patients who "got into their hands."

I said that in that case I assumed that if Robert had tonsillitis or earache the very last specialist to consult would be an ear, nose and throat man because he would be unable to recognise a healthy ear, nose or throat if he saw it, and we did not want Robert exposed to the danger of needless dismantling from the neck upwards. Therefore I would take him to a chiropodist for ENT disorders, a dentist for eye defects and possibly the vet for anything I was unable to put into a fairly wide spectrum of probabilities myself.

More than usually nettled, my father told me I was talking "abject rubbish" – which, of course, I was – but so was he, and that as far as co-educational schools went they would be disastrous and whatever I said etc., etc., etc., he could assure me he was right.

A satisfactory afternoon ended. I knew I had scored a victory, he knew he was right, and my mother was able to go home with a twitching, stiff upper lip, at having had to be the audience at a very 'unpleasant' fight – a 'fight' she had herself engineered.

We never again went to stay with my parents. We moved house, escaping from sumptuous Surrey and the particularly sumptuous bit of it we had inhabited – in my case off and on –where it was naturally assumed that the phrases "Well, probably see you at Ascot," – or Henley or Wimbledon – were prophesies meant seriously, and the discussions at dinner parties were often earnest exchanges of opinion concerning the best winter sports resort, so that, as usual, I felt I was on the outside looking in – but, for once, on a life I did not find enticing.

We moved to Beaconfield, to a much more varied and interesting town. It also meant that, unobtrusively, and without severing all links, we could restrict contact with my parents to tolerable proportions – tea on Sunday afternoons, lunch occasionally, sometimes both, but never more. I never overcame the fear that given time I might tell them exactly what I thought of them – a self-indulgence I was not prepared to risk. Moreover, I did not want to influence Robert's feelings for them. I once lashed out at my mother for interfering – she thought I was too casual about his food and said so, adding that she could not understand my detached attitude towards him. Her worst enemy, she said, could not accuse her of ever having been an overprotective mother but she was worried that I seemed perilously unconcerned about his food, bowels, tempers and feelings and I would, one day, regret it.

He grew tall, strong, independent, considerate, uninhibited and became an actor, musician and writer.

I once asked him if he had ever had any trouble with his bowels. He looked at me as though I were dotty. "Trouble with my bowels?" he asked. "Why, should I have?" I thought of the daily questioning of John and me. "Have you been properly?" pronounced for some obscure reason in that context, "proply." On a daily walk as small children, my brother had once said to me, "What's that in the road?" And I had replied: "Only horse's proply. It's nasty. Don't look."

My parents adored Robert, justifying their overt favouritism by constant reminders that he was their eldest grandchild and had spent so much of his babyhood in their house. He loved them too and we were determined that he would form his own relationships in life without any pressure from us. The bond between them was unsurprising. My mother had inexhaustible patience with him and would manoeuvre losing games of Snakes and Ladders and Ludo, finish off a barely begun strip of French knitting to be curled, eventually, into a mat for him to give me for Christmas, and read to him for hours. She only needed restraining from prancing in and out of the larder in frantic efforts to find something tempting for him to eat when he was not hungry. My father let him get away with crimes which, in our day, would have meant flogging, if not eviction, deportation, or even death by hanging. He compensated with unrestrained affection for all the injustices meted out to me as a child.

Robert could trample freely over my father's garden.

As children, John and I nicked a tulip in half with a ball. We ingeniously performed a grafting operation with matches and green cotton. To our embarrassment the casualty outlived its companions and eventually had to be stealthily de-petalled in the dark by my brother before my father, noticing a rebellious quirk of nature, inspected it more closely and discovered our wickedness.

When my parents visited our house, we played cricket in the garden. Robert was allowed to bat all the time, unless he decided he would rather bowl, at which moment one of us would disastrously miss a catch. The irony was watching my father batting in our garden. With furious energy and a total lack of respect for our flowers, windows and the neighbours' gardens he hit out madly in all directions, demolishing roses, decapitating tulips by the dozen, breezily ignoring the crash of glass of broken windows and yelling to the neighbours, "I say, just return the ball, will you?"

༄

We were in Oxford when Lally's second son was to be christened. My mother set off to go into Oxford by bus. Charles, of course, offered to give her a lift, not because it was raining hard but because it was his nature to be helpful. Her preference was to be a victim, so in spite of further pleas by Charles she insisted on martyrdom. After she left, my father reproved Charles bitterly for not giving her a lift, at which I lost my temper at the injustice. I followed my father to his study and attacked him physically, punching his stomach and beating my fists on his chest.

My stab at "being me" was uncalculated, unexpected and unavoidable. It might have been avoidable had it been calculated but it was so new and fresh, so innocently unforeseeable that to try to escape it would have been as useless as asking a two-year-old child to beat back a tidal wave. Nevertheless, I did try to evade it but my failure to do so remains the failure, the "giving in", the surrender in my life, which I shall never regret and which marked a turning point from which complete return would be impossible.

We went, son-less, in May to Majorca. A paradisal Majorca vibrating with the scent of roses, verbena, lemon trees, orange trees and wild flowers, the air wafted from the drift of angels' wings, the days spreading themselves out under the lavishly profligate sun, the nights a blue-black, velvet-warm display case for the stars and the within-arms-reach gentle mother-of-pearl moon.

All this beauty was there waiting for me with the

confidence, and the extravagance, of a country with unlimited resources to draw on – a climate so certain of sun, so sure of showers that expense on magic can be blithely disregarded. And I had flu. I was ill when we left home with aching back and head, and a throat so sore that anything I swallowed scratched its way down as if through emery paper. A holiday in the sun would clear it all up, I said. One day's sunbathing would act as a clarion call to my hosts of loyal, willing, antibodies all unobtrusively grouping themselves in readiness to cleanse me of invading, but disorganised, about-to-be-routed germs. A show of strength by my regiments of trained antibodies and victory would be mine.

However, the antibodies were dilatory. They were lurking, ready to spring, but they lacked initiative, had no sense of urgency. They kept me in bed and I didn't care a damn. I was convinced, anyway, that Majorca in May would be Scarborough in August, but with heat, in which the trippers could clutch their bottles of English tomato ketchup and Golden Shred to their bosoms and seek patches of shade in which to shield their varicose veins from the dangerous, foreign sun. The courier was aghast – she was missing her rake-off from organised tours and merrymaking in tatty nightclubs limbering up for the season. A doctor was called, muttered "pneumonia" – I think the only English word he knew – and sent a minion with injections for me. My recovery was so rapid that my fussily, pre-battle, square-bashing antibodies, forgetting military discipline launched themselves, half-trained, into Armageddon and within hours the illness slunk off, humiliatingly defeated.

I was the battlefield, though, and I felt as though I had been used as one. Where other people suffer a short period of mild post-flu depression, I swoop helplessly into at least a week of post-flu dark despair. I knew it would pass, but on that occasion it was wasting my holiday, money and time.

We went for a drive round the island. I could see it and smell it and I knew that it was the most beautiful spot in the world. I suddenly thought 'this is NOT post-flu depression. Even with flu I would respond to this loveliness but I am emotionally dead.' When we got back to the hotel I had a bath, intending possibly to go downstairs for dinner.

Before dressing, before even brushing my hair, I tottered out onto the balcony into the evening's caress of sunlight, testing my body for symptoms. The hotel was set in a tiny cove with a panoramic view of glittering sea, blackish green woods and hills vivid with wild flowers. I swivelled my eyes round in one bored, uninterested look, glanced down at the swimming pool and there, lazily swinging on a hammock seat was a Greek god. Very, very tall he was, with hair of such pale, pure gold that the golden sunlight deepened to crude copper in comparison. His body was tanned – not the purplish brown of the dark skinned – but the tawny leonine tan of the very fair. And as I glanced at him he smiled up at me. To no response. Dully my look travelled beyond him and then something made me look down at him again. He was still smiling up at me and his smile split through me like forked lightning, melted ice, woke every nerve and touched my heart. I had been dead and a fraction of time later, I was alive, warm, aware. I turned back into the room and said lightly, "I've made a hit" and laughed. I was better but not hungry or curious enough to go down to dinner. I lay down for an hour or so and when I thought everyone else would be dining, I went out on to the balcony again – not in search of my Greek god but to make sure of the view. From above me a very low, foreign, slow voice said, "Hullo". I looked up and he was there, smiling again, this time from his balcony one floor up. I answered, "It's a nice spot here," and that was that for that day. I thought no more of it. I was glad I was well again and hoped I might still enjoy a Majorca which was emphatically NOT Scarborough in August after all. I ordered a boiled egg to be sent up to my room and went early to bed looking forward to a lazy, sun-drenched holiday.

The next morning I dressed and went to the village store to buy beach shoes, returning just in time for lunch. I was normal again, perfectly normal, until I looked up – on the other side of the room, alone at a table, sat my Greek god staring at me, willing me to look his way. As I did so, he lifted his glass and drank to me. I was flattered and pleased. I giggled and repeated, "I HAVE made a hit." What I did not realise was that I myself had been hit. In a detached way I appreciated that he was the most beautiful human being I had ever seen. In a surprised way, I noted that it was odd that so young a man should notice me at all. I had had only what might be called three exceedingly brief encounters with him – all at a distance – and I meant to concentrate on grabbing the sumptuous luxury of sizzling in the sun.

That evening I went down to dinner for the first time since arriving in Majorca. We went to the bar first and were joined instantly by the young man. He was, it transpired, Danish, not Greek, and we had our drinks together. His English was good – slow, careful, sometimes lost for the right word, he talked about himself and also told us that there was dancing in the hotel every night. For the one and only time we knew each other I made a demand. I said, truthfully, that my husband did not like dancing and I hoped he, the Dane, would dance with me once that evening. Yes, he said, it would be a 'fine' pleasure for him and with that we all went in to dinner, he to his solitary table, ourselves to a table next to an English couple with whom we were striking up a slight, tepid, holiday friendship.

The minute the music started after dinner the Dane was bowing to me, asking for his dance. I felt uncomfortable at having demanded this favour – there was a crowd of young people who had invaded the hotel as they did, nightly, from hotels along the coast which were not even making an effort to get 'the season' under way. I deliberately danced, not badly – I can't – but formally and the second the record was over I patted him, dowager-like, on the arm, said, "Thank you very much. You have done your good deed for the day," turned my back on him and walked away. As I reached my chair, the music started again and there, looming over me, was the Dane, smiling into my eyes, holding out his hand and asking me how to ask me to dance with him in 'correct' English. "Just as you have," I said and that time I really danced.

We danced the whole evening. I suggested more than once that it would be more fun for him to pay attention to the girls in the hotel. He looked down at me, always into my eyes, and said very solemnly that he wanted to dance only with me. I believed him. I do dance well, of course, but we FITTED each other so well and gradually the dancing became less dancing than moving together as one person. I adored it and, when I went to bed, I hugged the thought to myself that I had had one, unique, perfect evening. I knew it could not be repeated but it didn't matter. It had happened to me and I would remember it.

However, the next morning I went onto the beach and there in splendid, truly magnificently splendid, isolation sat the Dane gazing forlornly, sadly at the horizon. I considered. I thought, he has seen me in the daylight from considerable distances, fully dressed. He has danced with me in near darkness fully dressed. I am now in a bikini and disillusionment is going to hit him right between the eyes. Sanity will be restored all round, I shall drive him to more suitable company and shall settle myself back into a cosier mood with my husband who, while not begrudging my Cinderella-like performance of the previous evening, had made it clear that he did not wish it repeated. I plonked myself beside the Dane and prepared to observe him reacting to the discovery of the Medusa whom he had mistaken for a pretty girl.

It didn't happen. When he saw me he smiled his wide smile, his eyes slanting upwards. "Tonight," he suggested, "we will dance again, every dance, and in the afternoon we will 'stroll?'" My husband joined us on the beach and I thought, this has got to be put into perspective. We have a lot of young friends whom we treat as sons when they visit us and this is how friendship has got to be. I criticised the Dane's English. He lapped it up. He wanted to improve his English. My husband glared at the sea and soon the Dane was glaring once again at the horizon too. I had upset them both and was glad when the Dane went off to bathe. My husband was not pleased with me and said so.

I could see his point of view but at the same time I had done nothing wrong. Being ticked off made me less sure that I wanted the Dane brushed aside. I wanted to spend my evening dancing with him. There was no harm in it and what had been, I told myself, a triviality became more important. The Dane came back, gathered up his towel and walked away. 'Damn,' I thought and was irritated by what I felt had been Charles's sulky attitude towards him.

By the evening I was refreshed and good-tempered. I had had my fun and we set about cementing the foursome with the other English couple.

The dancing started and with it came my Dane. I completely forgot my half-hearted resolutions and danced and danced with him and this time we talked, whispered, too. The minute he had seen me he had fallen in love with me, he told me. It was so long since I had heard the word "love" I was as shocked as I had been the evening he had brought me to life with his smile. When the dancing was over, he suggested a "stroll". Mad, irresponsible, young I was. I went. Mad, irresponsible young and incredulous when he kissed me. I forgot everything and kissed him too. We clung together and I responded as though it was "right", "good", "proper". Then, I remembered. I remembered who I was, where I was and realised what I was doing. I pushed him away. "No," I kept saying. "No. We must stop." He agreed, oh yes, he agreed. He was sorry. I was sorry. "But I LOVE you" he said, "I LOVE you" and I begged him over and over again to forgive me. I explained how I hadn't guessed that he had not just been enjoying dancing with me, as I had enjoyed dancing with him. I had not meant to 'lead him on'. I heard myself saying 'please understand' over and over again and that tall, fair god turned from me and leant against a wall, his face buried in his hands in a gesture of utter despair. I COULD not leave him. As I moved towards him he turned to me and there were tears in his eyes. "I am married," I said. "I have a son, I..."

"I understand," he said. "I like your husband. I understand, but PLEASE...I cannot help it," and I was enfolded again in his arms. I was kissed as I had never been kissed before, my body soft, yielding, limp in response to a strength and tenderness I had long since forgotten existed, even if I had ever really known it did.

Lying in bed that night I was slightly horrified and mildly

shocked by my behaviour, but the horror and shock was tempered with exhilaration and a conviction that in some way it had been "right".

The next morning I decided that I had had a glimpse of an answer to a great need but that my Dane, so to speak, having not had his "fun", everyone would settle back into order and their right places. After breakfast in bed we sought out the English couple and I set to consolidating the holiday friendship with them. We bathed together, lunched together and after lunch (no sign of the Dane) I sunbathed on our balcony. Later I dressed for dinner and was emerging from our room when I heard a very low soft voice at the end of the passage say "Hullo". I turned and he came towards me, a nerve twitching at the corner of his jawbone. I felt so weak at the sight of him I had to clutch at the wall for a second to keep my balance. Then I rallied and said brightly, "Have you had a nice day?" Very serious he was. He put his arm round my shoulders and said, "I went to Palma…but without you I was…tristesse. Tonight we dance. And tomorrow we go together to see the island, we go strolling."

After that night's dancing I thought to myself that if God were presenting me with SUCH a treat it would be churlish to refuse it. Then I told myself temptation was deliberately put in our way to turn our backs on. After that I decided that if there was a God and if He was going to torture me with such a cruel test of strength, I would say, "Right. I give in – it's wrong but I'm not wasting time arguing the toss with you – you are too devilishly devious for me." I simply abandoned any idea of ordinary holiday enjoyment and let myself be led wherever the Dane wanted to lead me. But first I had to make sure of him, make sure that I wasn't in fact making the fool of myself I suspected I must have appeared to be making. I put him to the test. I thought perhaps he was short of money and believed that all English women abroad were frustrated ladies with a great deal of money to spend on lovers. I told him that the allowance by our government for taking abroad was £50 and that I had already spent mine and had none left, even for drinks. His reaction? He asked me if I would like him to buy me a Majorcan pearl ring that would look "very good" on my dark, tanned hand. Unconsciously he revealed that he was not a womaniser – he had lived with the same girl for four years until she deserted him while he was away at sea for three months. That had been a year ago, since which he had not had more than casual, one-night stands with girls – a situation he gravely deplored as being "not for love". I asked him if the other young men in the hotel had got a wager with him that he wouldn't get me to bed with him. He was furious. Had I not seen that he was travelling completely alone? He had no friends in Majorca. If I said anything like that again he would put me across his knee and spank me. I said I simply could NOT understand what he was up to when there were so many girls on this island.

"Girls!" he said in the tone of voice a boy of five uses about the silly creatures.

I begged him not to be angry with me and he said he would

be angry if I didn't believe that he just loved me. I relaxed. He was good, through and through, that pure gold Dane. And having got all my suspicions out of the way I simply FELT and strangely, what I felt was not ecstasy but a warm, all-embracing contentment. The contentment I felt resulted in a blossoming of part of me I never knew existed. I ceased to be witty and sharp. For example, when he asked me if the other English couple spoke the 'high' English I did, I was surprised to hear myself saying very gently, "Well, perhaps not quite; they come from a different part of the country," and it was only after I returned to England and was reliving every moment of that halcyon time that I realised that to anyone else I would probably have said briskly, "Good God, no – straight from the gutter". He loved to hear me speak and mimicked perfectly my announcement to him that I spoke Oxford English, mimicking as well the proud lift of the head he said I had raised as I had told him. "I love your Oxford English – please tell me again about it." Again he mimicked the lifted chin, the 'proud look' as he called it.

He used to wait until I was alone in the small bar-cum-lounge of the hotel, walk past me and straight out into the road, up a winding slope and round a corner, and there he would stand until I arrived to nestle into him and we could wander through the woods and over the hills behind the hotel. He picked me flowers and once found, on top of a hill, a perfect shell – "a present from you to me," I said, and put it carefully in my cigarette case. We talked and talked and always returned to the same theme. He loved me. I loved him. And miles away in the country, we whispered, our voices hushed with the intensity of love. We laughed because our eyes were exactly the same colour and shape, and then he looked away from me and said, "I cannot talk. I cannot listen to you when I see you because I want you so much."

I said, "There will always be a corner of my heart reserved for you."

"I love you and shall love you with all my heart until I die," he said.

"So when you are an old, old man sitting in a corner watching your great-grandchildren playing, you will sometimes think of the English Lady in Majorca?" I asked.

"Not sometimes. Always. All my life," he said despairingly. And I was touched. The tiny bit of me which was left aware of my age smiled and sighed at the same time, because I knew that youth forgets and the memory of his English Lady in Majorca would fade, the wound heal, long, long before I had ceased to weep for him. And one stipulation I made we stuck to. I would not tell him my name and I refused to listen when he tried to tell me his.

For a time we stopped short of becoming lovers – just. He was strong and he was good. It seemed to me that we were so deeply in deep waters that the final surrender would be nominal, not worth the frustration and yearning and imagining that we were enduring. Then one day he laid his head on my breast and cried. As I smoothed his pale gold hair, hair thick and straight and soft as a butterfly's wing, it felt almost sacrilegious to touch it, I knew we must give each other everything we had before it was too late. Again, the tiny bit of me which had escaped him – the respectable, sensible married woman – had a sneaking suspicion, hope even, that we should fail each other and I should return unscathed to normality and he, disillusioned, would turn equally unscathed to a girl. The opposite happened. Our feelings, our bodies, our thoughts united and each time we met, every dance we danced, every moment we were together – and we were apart very little – love became more urgent. And I think everyone in the hotel must have felt it. And, oddly, approved.

There was a Danish couple in the room over ours and every time I went out onto the balcony, if they were there they threw chocolates down to me. I found that much more difficult to manage than the haphazard throwing away of my 'morality'. Hating chocolate, I used to pretend to put it in my mouth, walk into my room and toss it into the waste paper basket. Once, reading, while waiting for my Dane to pass me in the bar with the twitching jaw and glance that said, 'Follow me now,' I heard a waiter mutter to him, "The Señora is alone." The Dane gave the wretched little man such a look of freezing contempt I remonstrated with him later. "I love you," he said with glorious conceit. "It is not right for waiters to speak of you."

Once I opened my bag for a cigarette and, looking into it, he said, "Oh what disorganisation!" He had been in the navy and his bathing towel, sandals, anything he was carrying were always so tidy, folded with such precision that it was difficult to believe he was indulging in anything as untidy as an affair.

His room was the same – it looked almost uninhabited and yet we had such fun. It seemed that God himself as well as the hotel in general and the 'impudent' little waiter were aiding and abetting us. Behind the hotel, groves of trees, black-barked, blackly green-leaved, abounded everywhere and they all bore pods – a vast harvest of pods weighing down a profusion of trees. On one of our ambles, I asked the Dane if they were olives or almonds. He snatched a pod off a tree in passing and I said in mock anger, "How could you? That's stealing. You've ruined some peasant's entire crop of whatever it is not and you must PUT IT BACK AT ONCE." Laughingly he hung it over the branch and we continued our aimless wandering – aimless? Searching for a soft little bed of moss. When it was time to leave, he put his arm across my chest and hold me under my armpit as a father might a little girl in case she scampered off, while he carefully brushed me down and smoothed my hair. He had to bend over me for this and I would lean against his shoulder, loving the attentiveness, amused by his fatherliness, sometimes trying to wriggle away from him for the sheer delight of feeling his grip tighten, the brushing down firmer, the look of concentration on his face.

The next day I said I still wanted to know what the trees were, perhaps one pod among so many would not absolutely deprive a whole family of their livelihood. He stretched out his hand to take one and I said, "No, no, you must find the one you stole yesterday." "That could take a hundred years," he laughed. "I know it's not the tree we were near yesterday."

"Then we must comb the island," I said. "My bag may be in terrible disorganisation but we won't leave Majorca disorganised as well." I walked straight up to the nearest tree and there, exactly where it had been "replaced" was the missing pod! Carefully, he put it in his pocket saying "And that is your present to me – I shall keep it always."

⁂

I dutifully spent the mornings with Charles – but it was not a tiresome duty. Lying on the beach or beside the pool I was wrapped in happiness and, amazingly, I never had the tiniest doubt that the Dane would still be mine for the rest of the day – I who have always regarded happiness with niggling suspicion. I should have thought I would be tormented by jealousy, shaking with fear at the vision of the goddesses he might be meeting, resentful of every second spent away from him. On the contrary, I imagined his athletic graceful body water-skiing, devaluing in comparison his fellow-tourists on organised tours of the island, his forlorn expression caught off-guard, which would be dissipated at the sight of me. A prince, he seemed, accompanied always by a shadow of sadness which I alone could drive away, and I was beautiful, radiant, as I had never been before. I looked into the mirror and saw reflected a different me – a very feminine, glowing, ageless loveliness was there. I felt serene, integrated – almost smug. I used no make-up. And during those mornings, I never doubted for a second that the Dane would be waiting for me whenever I was ready. He was sure of me too. There was only one difficult hurdle for him. He had a conscience and once gloomily told me of his guilt at what he was doing to my husband. I thought to myself, 'Blast. Now I've got to bring my giant intellect to bear on a problem when all I want is just to "be".' "But he doesn't know and never will," I said. The Dane was not satisfied. Whether or not my husband knew was not the point. His English, normally so fascinatingly very slightly broken, almost deserted him.

"One of the lovely things is your 'clear' eyes. You are – yes – clear, I know it not, but he must be savage and he is a gentleman he seems." His English improved. "If you were my wife and we were in Denmark I should beat you."

I had a momentary vision of the delight of being 'spanked' by his large, authoritative, strong hand but I had put it aside to concentrate, unwillingly, on oiling the troubled waters of his puritanical conscience. The reward for my efforts was in sight, anyway – the lighting up of his eyes, the sombre frown removed, the wide, wide smile revealing even white teeth, the renewal of kissing, nibbling, caressing, searching for a so far undiscovered bit of me.

Cornered, I lied – semi-lied. "When you say 'clear' I think you mean honest, don't you?" I asked. "Well, the answer is not in black and white – it is grey. Do you understand? My husband and I have been married a long time. He does not want me as you want me and you are giving me something he cannot give me. If he knew everything he would understand. He is kind and gentle and it is not the time I spend with you he resents – if indeed he resents anything. He is self-contained, self-sufficient. I think he would rather not know but that is all."

As I predicted, this very potted but more or less truthful assessment of the situation was enough. My Dane listened very intently and as he listened I watched his face – the shadow of a cloud on a cornfield passed and then came the pure, wonderful smile, the face alive, eyes, gold-specked green sparked with happiness.

Again, mischievous angels must have giggled behind folded fluffy wings that day. We never DID manage to find the same mossy bed two afternoons running and that time we found ourselves in what appeared to be an endless forest of olive trees when suddenly we came to a clearing, a tiny patch of sunlit grass surrounded by trees. Why was it there? And why, oh why, miles from any house or cottage, was there, abandoned in the middle of it, an enormous, upholstered sofa? The Dane inspected it carefully. It was not very beautiful but its cover of beige moquette was clean; it was huge and I think we probably made the best use of the sofa it had ever known.

When we finally found our way out of the trees, we came to a very high wall edging the road. The Dane vaulted over it, turned, laughing to me and spread his arms to catch me. Instead I threw my bag into them. He bent quickly to put it at his feet and opened his arms for me again. My feet had been above his upturned, expectant eyes – the only time I ever looked down at him – and I jumped. He caught me as though I were thistledown and said, "So you are a ballerina – yes?"

During all those enchanted May time Majorcan days and nights I never once thought of the end. I simply obliterated days, dates and time from my mind. I think, at that time, if tragic news of fires, disasters or even deaths had arrived from England I should, like Scarlet O'Hara, have said to myself, "Oh, fiddle-dee-dee. I'll think about it tomorrow," so absorbed was I in living, in loving, in the absolute present.

Until the last day. Then we decided, my Dane and I, that we must have a very long time in a real bed together. I had never been to his room and furtively creeping, after lunch, to Room 555, deciding that if a couple we had talked with should appear on that floor and discover me, I should have to pretend that I had pressed the wrong button in the lift, I knew that I could never enjoy illicit love affairs as a way of life. I was scared. I didn't falter but flickers of fear darted round my heart, and when I reached his door I was shaking with apprehension as I opened it softly and shut it behind me.

He was standing with his back to the door but he saw me in the mirror. And that generous, gallant, chivalrous lover looked at my reflection, thinking that I could not see what he was doing. He was giving me time to change my mind, to escape, to leave him as though I had never been there. And his jawbone was twitching and I could see the desire in his eyes. It was my turn to say a tremulous "Hello" and he was across the room, holding me, and I was home. I think he was as unused to gallivanting in hotels as I was. It was I who thought of locking the door! Once together it was the culmination of our little lifetime, and when it was time for me to go neither of us could speak.

My last sight of him was the next day as we left the hotel. I looked out at the swimming pool, now sunless. He was swimming the length of it, underwater, over and over again, every now and then surfacing to shake water out of his eyes before submerging himself again in the comforting loneliness of his solitary bathe.

⁂

We returned to Beaconsfield to find it shimmering in sunshine. In the garden, roses bloomed early, butterflies fluttered and bees buzzed busily. Charles went back to work and I reclined, day after day, in the scented garden, French windows open, listening to records of the music to which the Dane and I had danced away the evenings in Majorca. My mood was a curious mix of heartbreak and happiness. Never for an instant, during the hours spent with the Dane, had the idea nudged me that this halcyon interlude might stretch beyond the two weeks we had together. Nevertheless, while luxuriating in reliving the affair, I did weep, now and then. I must have looked as a well-loved, tanned, post-holiday woman should look. I caught strangers looking at me admiringly and men wolf-whistled as I passed. At a dinner party, my table companion remarked that I had smiled a secret smile and asked what I had been thinking about. I thought Charles was working unusually hard, possibly to catch up after the break. I reproached him for being less 'amusing' and he said he often thought of witticisms but couldn't be bothered to voice them. That seemed mean-spirited...

I didn't consider confiding in a friend but I felt an urgent need to tell someone and made an appointment to see Dr Cohen. Her ploy was not helpful; it seemed to be to save my marriage by belittling the affair, calling the Dane "the lad" and the affair an "episode". As it turned out, she left London for an extended visit to Israel after a couple of sessions and I sought help from the psychotherapist, Dr Eilenberg, who had originally treated me in the Maudsley. I told him everything that had happened to me.

He suggested that it would be a mistake to wrap the affair in tissue paper as a treasured memory, that the longing for the Dane would be painful but that I might emerge to find the world had more Danes in it. He asked how Charles had taken it. Charles had seemed to me, at the time, perfectly happy for me to dance the nights away and to – as I lied to him – go off every day with the Dane to help him improve his English. I told Dr Eilenberg that Charles didn't know, to which he replied that, in his experience, the spouse always knew.

Some weeks later, believing that Chas had known all about

the Dane all along, I thought it would be better to discuss it openly and get back to normal. In doing so I wept, at which Charles's instinctive generosity took over and he said "I cannot get him for you. Don't ask me to."

Following my meeting with Dr Eilenberg, our lives returned superficially to normal with feelings of security and safety with each other, but sometimes I was conscious that I had changed in subtle ways. My mother was admitted to hospital suffering from pemphigoid, the illness from which she would die. I dutifully visited her every few days with a mental list of news and gossip. I found that having confronted, during psychotherapy, the damage I had experienced as a child, I was wary of confiding anything apart from trivialities in her. I managed to impart little bits of news about books I was abridging, Robert and Charles, and clothes, with an air of wanting to share with her the important details of my life.

❧

Eventually, my father telephoned one morning to say she had died. I drove down Maxwell Road in Beaconsfield singing to myself 'I'm free! I'm free!'

Some days later I attended her funeral at Headington, where Geoffrey had been cremated. After the service my father was determined to gather up all the cards that were attached to bunches of flowers and wreathes. The Chancellor of the University at that time was the tall, handsome Lord Halifax who arrived just as we emerged from the service. His chauffeur opened the boot of his car in which there were two or three wreathes, extracted one of them and handed it to Lord Halifax to lay among the floral tributes. There were obviously more funerals for the Chancellor to attend that day.

Whether or not Charles had had suspicions about what was happening with the Dane, he was now terribly wounded. Our lives seemed to be meaningless or, worse, tortured. Once driving somewhere we caught sight of a man we knew mowing his lawn and I felt Charles wince beside me. He was in emotional pain and I was emotionally numb.

At that time I barely read but the *New Statesman* was delivered as usual. Having glanced at it I threw it down and it opened on a column I had never before noticed. It consisted of advertisements inserted by people looking for people. Not pausing for reflection, I picked up my telephone and without working it out in advance said, "Beautiful Lady wants male shoulder to cry on. No ulterior motive." I had no idea that these messages were given box numbers for replies. I was astonished when, a short time later, bundles of letters tied up with elastic bands started landing in the porch, often with passport photographs attached. My letters, I heard, were in record numbers. I met several of the senders, always arranging to meet in public places and, from time to time indulged in the hopeless quest for gratification, either in London or, if Charles was away, in our own guest room. One of them was a reasonably well-known journalist who suspected I was some sort of spy – others were, for obvious reasons, lonely and friendless. My guilt was easily assuaged by my conviction that achieving a satisfactory sex life was my right. Finally an American, Truman Peebles, retired from the FAO of the United Nations, wrote to me. He was an environmentalist, living apart from, but still on affectionate terms with, an alcoholic wife, and with a son and daughter in London. We found we had many mutual interests and eventually decided that love was a need on both our parts and I should move in with him in London. We rented a small terraced house in Fulham and then I bought a flat in Bishops Mansions and furnished it with things brought from Beaconsfield. Meanwhile Charles sold our Beaconsfield house and bought a cottage there. We were very friendly on the occasions when we had to meet and he was very generous to me financially as well.

Truman was a clever, satisfying and devoted lover. He was also unusually interested in psychology. This interest was focussed on me and was not only flattering but also encouraged me to express past and present feelings with a freedom not previously experienced other than in consulting rooms. We spent time with his wife, son and daughter in their house in Fulham. As an incentive suddenly to become teetotal, meeting Truman's wife, Maybelle, was a stark warning of the evils of drink. His son Pat, an inventor, was living with an English girlfriend, Dikla, the daughter of writers and herself a gifted participant in numerous artistic activities. Dikla was not only intelligent with a warm personality, she welcomed me into this American group as a fellow foreigner and we became affectionate friends. Friends who included my BBC producer, Pat McLaughlin, for whom I continued working as an abridger. John and Dr Eilenberg, to whom I had unburdened myself about the Dane, met Truman and approved of him. Most important of all was Robert's visit from Manchester to meet Truman and check on Charles's welfare. Both inspections were completely satisfactory. I mentioned Truman to Lally and said Chas and I were separated. What did she think? She said she was working out what to have for supper.

During the time spent with Truman, Chas and I sometimes had to meet at weddings and funerals, and it was at a funeral that a feeling I had had for some time came strongly to the fore. I had become irritated by Truman's constant interpretation of what lurked behind everything I said. Sometimes he understood my subconscious needs with astonishing insight, but I needed a little emotional privacy.

While living with Truman, my father died. Unlike the feeling of freedom I had had when my mother died, I felt nothing at all when it was his turn. I wondered whether he might have cut me out of his will but he had left everything fairly divided between the three of us – though, in fact, long before he died he had given Lally a farm in the Lake District, which came via my godmother, Mrs Maude. In financial and emotional terms, he always favoured her. Her attitude towards him had always been instinctive and subconscious – in no way calculated – but it ensured that she would maintain her status as the best loved daughter and so enjoy her just rewards.

In Oxford after his funeral, Chas and I were alone together. The familiar sight of him, his pleasure in seeing me and the familiar, soft, slightly Irish tone of his voice, were irresistible. We found ourselves in each other's arms and I felt completely safe and secure, as though finally reaching home after a peculiar adventure. He wanted me back, which was where I wanted to be; but there was Truman to be considered and we had to pause and think. Back in Fulham with Truman I was in emotional turmoil, which he was aware of, and with gentleness and consideration he observed my inner conflict, and though longing for me to stay with him, and telling me so, he refrained from appealing to me or reproaching me. It took weeks to resolve the situation, but finally Truman moved out of the flat and I was no longer the object of continuous scrutiny. In due course Charles moved in. While we had been apart, Chas had had an affair with a woman he had met on holiday. She was more or less happily married so they would meet between her home and Beaconsfield. She was anxious to continue in the same way, so Chas and I agreed to have a kind of open relationship, *à la* the Bloomsbury Group, and I would carry on spending time with Truman. The arrangement, predictably, did not last, but amazingly we all, with the exception of Charles's Marjorie, who rapidly disappeared, remained on truly good terms.

Once, during one of their trysts, Marjorie asked Charles what on earth would happen if he suddenly broke a leg or died of a heart attack when they were together. "Oh, just leave me alone and go home as if nothing had happened," he said. The flat was too small for us, and for Robert when visiting us from Manchester, where he was reading drama. We needed a larger house with room for antiques, his family silver and pictures, with a garden and, being Irish, his preference was for one with a basement, complete I said, with rats and cockroaches. Having had many English ex-public school boyfriends in Oxford, none of whom had lasted very long, Chas's slight Irish brogue and, above everything else, his total lack of self-consciousness, almost wildness, when thinking and acting unconventionally, was irresistible.

During a slump in the housing market, I noticed a For Sale board outside a house in Holmead Road, Fulham, where, as usual when driving anywhere vaguely unfamiliar, I had taken a wrong turning. We went to view it the next day and loved it. It even had an extension, a studio the length and breadth of the house under the roof – just right for Robert and his music. When we asked the price, Charles was instantly hopelessly downhearted; after the sale of his cottage and my flat, we could not possibly afford it, at which I uncharacteristically had an attack of optimism and suggested offering what we could afford, namely half the asking price. Charles refused to make a fool of himself to that extent, until I pointed out that he need not divulge his name so it really wouldn't matter how hilariously the house agent laughed.

He did telephone and it so happened that the house,

recently converted from a two-up two-down cottage, was now owned by the bank. The offer was immediately accepted and our rapture was only marred by the thought that a quarter of the asking price might have been enough.

Robert, now living in Camberwell unless working away from home in theatres or films, was always the focus of our interest and some of his friends became our friends as well. Almost as close as a brother was Mick Ford, whose partner, Rudi Davies, became my friend and confidante.

We felt that we were starting again and it was comforting. With easy access to the ENO, theatres, galleries and cinemas and no longer commuting from Beaconsfield, Chas could leave at a civilised hour in the morning and be home in time for three games of Scrabble every evening while, presumably, other people settled down to drinks before dinner. We played in the kitchen and occasionally were so absorbed in our games that saucepans of vegetables burnt so badly we had to start cooking again.

Our lives were on an even keel and we were back to our old habits of amusing each other, discussing the news, watching TV and making plans for holidays. There was only one thing missing – a sex life. After Robert was born, postnatal depression was the enemy, followed by my nervous breakdown, which meant Charles's role was more one of looking after a very ill wife than that of a husband. The Dane, followed by Truman, had opened my eyes to my needs and I realised that for me a meeting of minds was ultimately more important than sexual passion. However, when faced with an emotional jigsaw, I consulted Dr Cohen who suggested joining a group of couples with marital problems. Dr Robin Skynner, the doctor in charge, allocated us to a Dr Demari, an overweight, elderly psychiatrist who sat, hands clasped over his stomach, nodding like a Buddha while unhappy couples metaphorially sat at his feet, hoping that solutions for their disharmony would be worked out. Chas quite liked Buddha but I mistrusted him. I sensed that he was more supportive of the husbands, who admittedly were likely to be the wage-earners but which I thought was irrelevant. The way he responded to some of the problems presented to him was with a high-pitched giggle, which, he explained, was his reaction to the dynamics of the group.

While we were regular attendants, I had a blow when I lost my job, selling advertising space in glossy programmes sold at Charity events, in which I excelled. I thought it would be helpful to mention it at a group meeting, but it was swiftly passed over by Buddha. A few sessions later, one of the wives who had hardly spoken committed suicide. Shortly after that we stopped going to the meetings.

We decided to take a holiday. One night as we were going to bed, I said half-heartedly to Chas, "I suppose we ought to be trying to make love again," to which he replied, "Oh no! After all, we ARE on holiday!"

Our feelings for each other, now there was no longer that dissatisfied undercurrent, were deep and warm and, oddly, tactile. We appreciated our understanding of each other but I was concerned that we were so content that we had few close friends in London. I wondered how one of us would cope alone after the other one died – not a serious worry since I was older than Chas so he would be the one left. Chas was on an even keel, without cracks and crevices in his character. If I was late coming home, Chas assumed that I was in a traffic jam or queuing at a check-out. Should he not be at his desk if I rang him at the office, I imagined he had been in a fatal car crash, had lost his memory or had been rushed to hospital with a suspected heart attack. Within the next hour I would speak to his secretary to be told he had not yet arrived. Half an hour later, she would suggest I went to a neighbour if I was so bothered, or even that I should telephone the police. Five minutes after that Chas would telephone me to say he must have forgotten to mention that he might be delayed getting into ICI as he was going to a meeting first. Finally, I stopped panicking by recognising that panic was a crossroads for me. I could either assume that the lights were against him as he drove to Holborn or I could take the dark route leading to accidents, disaster, catastrophe or death.

Charles's unconventional outlook and unawareness of being observed by other people led to some entertaining scenes. I complained that I didn't like a bush he had planted at the end of the garden. He was about to leave for an important meeting with the chief executive of a distinguished company and was wearing a pinstriped suit and carrying a brief case and neatly rolled umbrella. He immediately leapt down the garden shouting, "Ah so, Ah so!" to the offending shrub and demolished it with the crook of the umbrella.

An even more useful trick was when we joined the end of a long queue to reach a drinks party at Liberty's in celebration of the start of the Christmas shopping spree. Chas instructed me to stay where I was, strode to the front of the shop, peered into it, glanced back at me and waved, calling "They're here, they're here!" and I was able to bypass the queue and go straight in with him.

※

Charles was generous and compassionate towards Geoffrey's parents and agreed that I should maintain a warm relationship with them. From time to time they came to stay with us in Beaconsfield, and Chas had heard from me the five-limbed saga of the Hipwells and the example they set for keeping bad news in perspective. One morning, a letter from Yorkshire told me that Mr Hipwell had died and the funeral had taken place. "Oh well," said Charles when I told him, "there wasn't much of him to go, was there?"

Chas brought me breakfast in bed each day before leaving for work and when I went downstairs any letters of interest would be on the kitchen table.

When Robert was at the Leys School in Cambridge, which he hated and about which we were worried, we had a begging letter from the headmaster, A Barker, asking for donations from parents towards the cost of a new science lab. We considered ignoring it, but were concerned about the effect the lack of support might have on Robert, so Charles duly sent off a modest contribution.

A week or two later, there was a formal acknowledgement and under his signature, in nearly illegible handwriting, was scribbled, "Bit mean wasn't it?" with the initials AWB scrawled beside it. I was astonished. The cheque, though not over-generous, had been for a reasonable amount and I took the letter to show Lionel Jeffries, an actor friend.

Lionel read it and, shouting with indignation, said it was outrageous, scandalous, and he was going to ring Barker that minute and tell him what he thought of him and his disgraceful reaction to a gift to the school.

I thought that Lionel's reaction was suitable, but felt that a call to the headmaster, not even from a parent, might not be in Robert's best interests and I managed to restrain him. When Chas came home that evening and I told him of Lionel's reaction to the postscript, he was amazed that I had been so gullible and delighted that the tease had been such a success.

Chas left the housekeeping money on the kitchen table on Mondays. On one occasion, I left him a note saying that if he didn't increase the allowance I would have to go on to the streets. When I went down later, there was a message from him at the end of mine saying, "Try it!"

☙❧

Beaconsfield was not boring but our lives were uneventful, as were those of other families in the outer suburbs as they trundled through time. Charles commuted to London daily while I waited impatiently for producers to offer me books to abridge for broadcasting. The final abridgements had to be cut into fourteen-minute episodes for serials going out in the *Woman's Hour*, *Afternoon Stories* and *Book at Bedtime* slots.

Robert came home at weekends and on one of his visits our lives changed dramatically. After meeting some of his Beaconsfield friends, he brought to tea a stranger who appeared to be on the periphery of the group, a boy called Chris Gislingham. Chris was exceptionally goodlooking but had a forlorn expression which interested me. Robert told us later that Chris was moving from one friend to another in Beaconsfield, usually sleeping in the backs of their parents' Minis. His good looks, warmth and appreciation of our hospitality had charmed us and we told Robert that we might offer Chris shelter for a night or two sometime if he was desperate.

Snow gripped Beaconsfield and I was abridging to the usual deadline. Charles and Robert were at a football match so I went early to bed to work on an abridgement, with enough space for papers and my typewriter beside me. I cut out words, transposed sentences from one chapter to another and reduced dialogue thus emphasizing the gist and pace of the book so that when read by an actor it would be attention grabbing.

My producer was Pat McCloughlin who, knowing my work and because I always met her deadlines, had commissioned me. Chas and I became close friends with her and after her mother died she moved from Sidcup to London into a flat just up the road from us in Fulham. The evening Chas and Robert were at the match and I was muttering excerpts from the book to test it for radio listeners, the doorbell rang. I answered it and a snow-covered Chris staggered into the porch begging for bread. I took him in, fed him and gave him a bed for the night. That night was the first night of the two years Chris lived with us, during which we were fascinated, maddened, and committed to caring for him with a mixture of affection and irritation.

I decided he needed to lie fallow for a time and refrained from urging him to find work, somewhere to live or even to get up in the morning before he felt like it. Charles and Robert were content with the arrangement although I was constantly advised by friends and neighbours to insist that he scoured the town for somewhere else to stay. Having embarked on the challenge of rescuing Chris from life as an unwelcome guest in the backseats of cars we had then to reorganise our own lives as required for the roles of unofficial guardians.

One morning soon after Chris arrived I was in bed working on a book when a young man was shown into my room by our cleaning lady. He was a Probation Officer who had a file on Chris.

He came over as someone accustomed to discussing his cases with strange women lying down crossing out passages in books, and he sat on the bed as I suggested. He told me he had come to me for help on Chris's behalf. Chris was due to appear a few days later at the Magistrate's Court regarding an escapade in which he had been caught driving a car in an erratic fashion. Despite being under age and without a license, the Probation Officer hoped that he could arrange for Chris to be "let off", possibly with a warning, if I would undertake responsibility for him, to which I agreed. Having patted ourselves on the back for removing the threat of punishment for Chris we had problems when woken up in the night to deal with demands for entry, raids on the larder and curses muttered by Chris trying not to disturb us.

Months passed util we noticed that we were no longer having to open the door for him in the night. He had found s stepladder in the garden shed and was able to climb up to Robert's bedroom window without knocking tiles off the sloping roof below, as had happened during previous attempts. Charles then gave him a latchkey which was continually forgotten or lost and so that it could no longer be slipped into a trouser pocket had to be tied to a large plank kept in the outside lavatory beside the back door.

Chris's parents were divorced. His father, the film director John Gilling, lived in Spain and his mother had remarried a Dr

Hornibrook. She suffered from depression so her doctor husband taught her how to inject herself with drugs. One night she called Chris to fetch her a glass of water. That was the last time he saw his mother alive.

Next morning his brother-in-law found her dead in bed having pierced an artery when injecting herself.

Chris and his sister and her husband were immediately evicted from the family home in Beaconsfield by their stepfather, thus leaving the coast clear for the local medics to rally round with sympathy and, more vitally, offers of professional support in view of his involvement in her tragic death. This happened when Chris was in his early teens. He had to leave Wellington, he ignored Wycombe Grammar School and found a haven with us. He told me his story during the first weeks and months of staying with us.

Much much later, facing a life in penury, he decided to sign up with Vidal Sassoon to train as a hairdresser. He drove with Charles to London daily and on qualifying decided he wanted to live on his own in London, an idea which we backed with alacrity.

After we moved to Fulham we saw more of Chris because I found a basement flat for him in a house overlooking Eel Brook Common, which we had discovered in response to an appeal from Geneste Holliday with whom I was a close friend. Her doctor daughter, Vicky, and Vicky's doctor husband needed a house in London while working at St Thomas's Hospital. Their lodger, Chris was an intriguing element in their lives with his retinue of adoring girlfriends.

Chris subsequently left Sassoon to work at the Barber Shop in Park Close, Knightsbridge. The shop was exactly as it had been in the early twenties with wood panelled walls painted dark green and the original black leather barber's chair. Chris and Michelle, a young French woman, were the stylists, with Jackie, a Jamaican, their shampoo girl. Charles and I, as well as many American tourists visiting London, were enchanted by the antiquity of the shop in the narrow passage of Park Close, so much so that when Chris called one evening Chas said that if ever the Barber Shop was up for grabs "Janet will buy it".

Soon after that the Barber Shop was for sale and Charles kept his word and I became the very surprised owner of a business venture which I had no idea how to manage. I had free hair-dos and visiting it was fun.

Jackie who was by far the most efficient and practical of the three of them and who also had a wit and warmth that was beguiling shampooed me, and Michelle did the rest. The atmosphere was informal and a number of clients were what we called theatrical riffraff and celebrities. Lord Scarman lived in one of the apartments in the Close and Chris cut his hair. He told Chris that Mrs Thatcher would go down in history as a great prime minister, adding "but I dislike her intensely". Once, when shaving a well-known journalist, Chris nicked his cheek from which oozed a drop of blood so he asked Jackie to fetch a piece of loo paper from the basement – "Unused" I called as she disappeared.

The financial side of the Barber Shop was a mystery. Occasionally Chris would invite us out to dinner and turn up for once without a girlfriend, reeking of aftershave and looking devastatingly handsome.

He would have reserved a table at a pricey restaurant and we would have a luxurious evening. The lavish hospitality bill and generous tip would be settled with cash from the Barber Shop till, which should rightly have been paid into the Barber Shop account for my disposal, probably on an antique or a seasonal necessity from Jaeger.

The fun didn't last. An income tax demand arrived and Charles and I were invited to a meeting at a tax office where the inspector turned out to be the sort of early middle-aged mousey woman who would go unnoticed wherever she went.

Subsequently we realised that she had actually been observed sauntering about in Park Close and peering into the shop. The meeting with this lady started with offers of tea and developed into an inquisition regarding the non-existent shop accounts, which bank held the account, whether I accepted cheques and cash, even, I remember, where I lunched.

The lunching question was easy. I knew the answer. "At my kitchen table listening to the radio," I said. She wanted to see my cheque stubs, some of which I had filled in. Charles's chequebook was also inspected with a question about a regular payment for a three initialled recipient.

We guessed she hoped it was the Barber Shop's bonus in appreciation of his help, the initials being those of a lady-friend. Charles was flummoxed until he remembered the initials were those of his (male) osteopath.

We emerged from the very long interview and stood on the pavement agreeing that we could imagine confessing to brutally murdering people we had never heard of in order to escape from the Lady Tax Inspector. The result of the meeting was that I was taxed several thousand pounds. It was clear that the Barber Shop was going to ruin me financially so I sold it, and Chris was furious until much later he realised that he could become an actor, which he had always yearned to be.

I interpreted the ambition as seeing himself descending the steps of aeroplanes, signing photographs of himself, waving to fans with the latest glamorous, as yet not-about-to-have-an-abortion girlfriend clinging to him. It was a wicked injustice on my part. He went to acting school, leading to a successful career as the actor Christopher Gilling. He has also enjoyed a successful career as a highly desirable man about town by taking the advice of his sister to "live as though you have money, even if you haven't." He has always been appreciative of how we helped him, but after the sale of the Barber Shop without consulting him our relationship broke up into an icy silence which was only subsequently reformed when he telephoned with news of a play in which he was taking a leading role. Since that play he has been a valuable and entertaining friend and by knowing Chris I have been forced to face the sad fact that I am a complete and total failure in the business world.

There were no more dramatic episodes as we resumed our ordinary lives. We went to the West Indies every winter for two or three weeks, once Charles had discovered that I could travel in the cheap seats at ICI's expense. We visited relations in Ireland. One year we decided to try something different and found an enticing offer of three weeks for the price of two in the Gambia. On arrival, we were hardly reassured by a Red Cross Clinic notice over a door in the reception area. Our room was adequate, but when we went down to the beach we found it was only the breadth of the hotel because, we were told, the rest of it was a highly dangerous part of the Gambia. I gathered that if you escaped drowning, you were risking robbery with violence.

After a week of indigestible meals, stomach upsets and visits by a doctor, we decided to apply for early release. The management was quick to point out that we would not be able to claim for the lost week; we refrained from offering a bribe to let us go and came back to cold, healthy London.

☙❧

After one of our visits to Ireland, Charles announced on the way home that he thought we might buy a cottage in the west of Ireland for weekends and holidays. I pointed out that travelling to it would take about three days there and three days back. If he wanted a cottage anywhere, France would be a better bet as it would be about half the distance, with approximately a five hour journey each way.

Not having realised that he had been listening, I was astonished when during the next few days he booked tickets to go to France by ferry to look for cottages in the Calais area. We bought a cottage in Fillièvres after several visits, some accompanied by a very enthusiastic Robert.

On a cold, wet, windy morning in October, Chas returned from the shops looking not only tired, but very drawn – almost shrunken. He told me how nasty it had been out, which was not the sort of thing about which he usually complained and asked me to go to the kitchen to listen to Radio 4, which he had switched on when he came in. Charlotte Greene was reading the news. Charles asked me if the radio sounded normal, making sense, or if it sounded peculiar. It didn't. He seemed relieved and we had lunch. For the rest of the day he appeared quite well but that night he suddenly woke up with what he described as an absolutely splitting, piercing, headache.

It lasted only a short time and the next day he was the same as usual until the evening, when we were driving to Hammersmith to attend some sort of political meeting and, as we passed Charing Cross Hospital, Chas said something about feeling a bit "off" about the headache. The sight of a hospital made me take him very seriously and he promised to go to the doctor the next day.

I suggested cutting the meeting, but he thought that as we were half way there we might as well carry on. The meeting was dull, as local political meetings tend to be, I was preoccupied with worry about Chas and he was clearly not making much effort to attend to any of it, so we agreed to leave.

The next day Charles, as promised, went to his GP, Dr Brass, whom he had only previously visited for jabs before travelling abroad on ICI oil business. As time elapsed, I decided to go to meet him but when I arrived the consultation was still in progress. When Chas emerged and saw me, he said Dr Brass would like to see me as well. Dr Brass who, unhurriedly, took time to discuss and advise us, referred Chas to a neurologist, Dr Zilcher, at the Cromwell Hospital and an appointment was arranged within the next day or two.

Robert by now knew what was happening and was deeply concerned. He was not only emotionally supportive, but also coped with practical problems as well. He telephoned Pat McLaughlin, my BBC book producer to tell her I would be unavailable to abridge a book for the present and explained why.

I remember that particular incident so clearly because we had become very close friends with Pat and when she rang me to ask for bulletins, she said how terribly upset Robert had been when he rang with the news. He dealt with and became telephone-friendly with Norwich Union regarding medical fees. He contacted Irish relations and other friends and relations. For Charles and me he was always companionable, helpful and calm, even amusing, so none of us lost our lightness of touch and wit. The sadness was very often spiced with sudden laughter and sparkle.

Chas had a biopsy. It revealed a brain tumour which could not be treated surgically. We took a photograph of him smiling and pointing out with his index fingers the side of his forehead where there was a scar left by the biopsy. He was courageous but more than that he wanted the truth, to face it and have as much control over any suggested treatment as possible.

The outlook was grim. The only medicine came in the form of pills. He was not in pain but the position of the tumour affected his speech so, although he could understand nearly everything we said to him, he could not always find the right words with which to speak to us. But as he was highly articulate, he was adept at hitting on alternatives – for example, glancing at the neighbours' cat in our garden, he said, "Look, there's that *person*." He could still read and once came back from the Cromwell with an article that had caught his eye to read to us. He was a music lover, with a passion for opera, especially Wagner. One evening, after we had listened to *The Flying Dutchman*, he analysed phrases from it so fascinatingly that the illness was, for the moment, forgotten.

∽⚬∾

Charles knew he was dying. Robert and I knew Chas was dying. We all reacted in different ways. Robert left his own house in Camberwell. He abandoned his normally very active social life and was unavailable for work, and moved in with us. I concentrated on the indestructible bonds between Chas and me that were so deep that this conscious emergence of them was, in a sense, comforting. We discussed everything that had happened during our marriage and Chas not only forgave me for my betrayal of him when I went to Truman, but actually said it had been "good for us".

Now and then I cried in his arms in bed, and once, with the difficulty he had with words, he managed to tell me that after he died I was not to be like Dickens's Miss Haversham hopelessly waiting, waiting.

Chas himself was supportive in emotional and practical ways.

He wanted us to know that he was not afraid of dying, and that we could talk about it openly.

Knowing that dealing with his affairs would soon become impossible, he asked Peter Shaw, our solicitor, to call on us. They went to Charles's study and when they rejoined us they had examined all Charles's files and were able to reassure us that everything was in order. Chas added, touchingly, to Peter that I was being wonderful, and Peter agreed that he was sure that I was.

Chas was transferred from the Cromwell, where he had been an inpatient for a month, to the St John & St Elizabeth Hospital. We knew the time was approaching when it would not be possible to look after him at home, so Robert and I had been investigating hospices. It is generally assumed that older couples live in a flat and that implies one floor and a bathroom on the same level. At home, without a cloakroom on the ground floor, he would have to negotiate two flights of stairs and he was steadily becoming physically weaker.

We inspected hospices that aimed at a homely look, furniture donated by grateful relations of patients and pleasant nurses in ordinary clothes. When we asked about music, we were assured that local choirs frequently came in to entertain the patients. We had hoped for enough privacy for Chas to listen to the music he loved.

We were sure that Charles would be happier in a conventional hospital environment, which was exactly what we found at the St John & St Elizabeth Hospice in North London – but not yet. In the meantime, he was in and out of the main hospital and Robert helped him with the stairs at home. We were all finding life exhausting and thus it was that I welcomed the suggestion that we should have a Macmillan nurse for one night.

Chas would be two floors up in his own bed with me, having taken sleeping pills, beside him, and Robert could have an undisturbed night, one floor above us. The nurse would be on call in the dressing-room with its own bathroom on the first floor. In the middle of the night, Charles went to my bathroom and collapsed on the floor. There was no response to our call for the nurse so Robert went to fetch her and she, of the four of us, was sleeping soundly in the dressing-room.

Robert helped Chas back to bed. The nurse stood looking at us, observing that we looked like a honeymoon couple, and then told me, helpfully, that marvellous nappies were now available for men. Chas was not, and wouldn't be, incontinent and he did understand everything that she said.

I had always believed that Macmillan nurses were not only highly trained in practical nursing, but were also picked for their empathic approach to the anxious families and friends of the patients. The next morning she was, I suppose, attempting to fulfil this delicate role. She had talked to Robert, heard that he lived alone in Camberwell and must therefore, she said, move in with me in Fulham.

This was not so much advice, more of an order. I was so stressed then that I barely restrained myself from telling her what I felt about her night nursing skills and her obtuse efforts to interfere with any arrangements I might make with Robert.

I was well aware of how incredibly bereft and alone I was going to feel, but it never occurred to me to think of sharing my house with anyone else, least of all Robert who was already sacrificing his freedom to help us while he was needed so desperately. I knew then and would always know that living together was out of the question for us both.

I knew also that I would be in desperate need of contact with the outside world and, above all, with friends and relations, so I spent a great deal of time telephoning and also begging to be telephoned.

Of my own family, it was typical that Lally, who couldn't

respond to emotional needs, was silent, whereas John rang frequently with medical advice on the treatment of brain tumours. The Irish friends and relations were, of course, shattered and constantly and sympathetically begged for news.

※

Chas went into hospital over Christmas and the New Year. On January 1st, I was asked to report to a very senior nurse. I assumed that I had ignored some hospital rule. To my astonishment, the meeting was requested for heartfelt apologies to be expressed for the appallingly lax care which had enabled Chas to climb out of his window and down to the street below, there to mingle with the New Year's Eve revellers. The police had returned him to the hospital. Robert was delighted to hear of Charles's agility and spirit.

During his stint in the hospital he was persuaded to have radiotherapy, which he absolutely hated and he refused to endure a course of it. The therapist came to see us, sitting on Chas's bed and explaining, sympathetically, that it was the only treatment available. Initially, I was in favour of anything which might prolong his life, but when told that the extended time would last only for about eighteen months, after which he would be back to where he was before the treatment, I was not so hopeful about its benefits.

Chas was adamant that dying was the preferable option, so

Robert and I were determined that no radiotherapy should even be suggested again.

Charles was rattled enough by the episode to need frequent assurances by us that he would die without further unwanted treatment.

Early in the New Year Chas went into the hospice, where the nurses wore nurses' uniform and there were polished floors and hospital beds. The doctor in charge was Dr Philip Jones, who listened to us attentively, understood us and was very gentle. Chas shared a room with one or two other patients. He was much happier there with no pressure to undergo treatments. He came home as often as possible, but it was difficult for Robert to help him up and down stairs and Chas was aware of the problems. He understood everything that was going on but was unable to join in conversations because of his struggles with words.

But we still laughed. One day, we were in the dressing room when he pointed to the nearly finished loo roll in his bathroom, wanting me to supply a new one. "Oh, Chas," I said. "I hoped that one would see you out." It was an example of the black humour we shared and being so apposite now it amused us both.

After a particularly difficult weekend with Robert struggling to help him, he started singing *Hey Jude* and, pointing at the stairs, asked to be taken back to the hospice. He meant that he would feel happier there and the singing was to show that that was what he wanted us to do for him.

Charles never lost his knack of finding life interesting. There was a voluntary helper serving coffee in the hospice, and Chas noticed the man was wearing a Trinity College tie. There was a well-known history don at TCD, Dr McDowell, who had a falsetto voice and an extremely strong Irish accent. He was mimicked by everyone in Dublin who ever met him. With whatever words he could muster, Chas addressed the Irish volunteer in Dr McDowell-speak and the volunteer responded delightedly and appropriately...

Robert and I went to the hospice directly after breakfast until the evening to be with Chas every day. We lunched in the canteen and nipped to the bank and shops for necessities. Back with Chas, we read the paper and solved the crossword together so that Chas need not try to talk but was not alone. We walked with him along the passages, and were able to do little things for him – cutting his nails and including him in chats with the nurses. We watched him become weaker and weaker until he could no longer feed himself and needed more and more professional nursing.

The sadness and dread I felt was overwhelming. One evening we knew, or were advised, to stay the night. I lay down while Robert sat up with Chas. I was dozing when Robert came and told me to come to Chas. I held his hand and cradled his head, telling him how much I loved him, his breathing became rasping and then stopped, and he died.

A doctor was sent for to certify his death and pat me on the shoulder, a nurse offered me tea in a side room and then, I suppose, we came home. We had to tell people about Chas dying, and arrange the funeral, which was to be a humanist service. A humanist came to see us and listened sensitively to our accounts of Chas's personality, achievements and interests, which were subsequently described at the cemetery where Chas was buried in a grave where there is room for me when needed.

Janet and Charles in the USA, on their last holiday before Charles died.

Robert and Charles Hickson on the last visit to the French cottage in Fillièvres before Charles died.

Art Rubino and Janet in Midhurst.

Truman Peebles and Zuni the cat.

Chris Gislingham.

Robert Charles Fitzgerald Hickson.

Kate Duchêne.

Anna Hickson.

Kate, Charlie, Anna and Robert at home in Camberwell.

Janet Hickson in 2009.

After Charles died, I wanted to die as well. I couldn't believe I could survive without him from a practical point of view, and much, much worse, life seemed completely uninteresting. Books had always been my lifeline but I couldn't be bothered to read. Music was much too painful to listen to and I didn't feel ready for a social life.

I had friends in Holmead Road on whom I was always welcome to call, but once Robert had moved back to Camberwell, the emptiness of my life was unbearable, so coming home after going out emphasised my desolation.

Two episodes at this time stand out in my memory. One of the hospice nurses who had been especially good with Charles had always seemed not unfriendly toward me but not as friendly as the rest of the nurses. The nurses worked in shifts and after Chas died, I felt she had decided that I wasn't taking the situation seriously enough. She may have thought I was calling in on Charles between lunches and drinks parties because I dressed as carefully as I always have. Charles would have noticed had I appeared without any of the rings or earrings he had given me over the years.

Dr Jones asked us to visit him for a meeting after Chas died and driving over there I told Robert that I would tell Dr Jones about the coolness of the nurse. Robert disapproved of this idea, but I decided to tell Dr Jones when there seemed a good moment to do so. As always, Dr Jones listened and understood and also understood my theory about the nurse. That night, the unfriendly nurse telephoned me to ask how I was, to say how much she appreciated Charles and looking after him, and she very much hoped that the heartbreak I was feeling would ease. She was warm and caring, and I was glad I had told Dr Jones who had probably suggested that it was wiser not to judge by appearances alone.

The other episode concerned my own family.

Robert went back to Camberwell, and I was in a state of almost paralytic grief and loneliness. I decided that this was a time when I might be able to respond to some family emotional support instead of being so dependent on Robert. I invited Lally and John to come to London to see me for a day. I picked them up at Paddington and when we sat down at home for drinks before lunch, John immediately launched into a tirade of criticism about Charles. According to John, Charles had had no friends (in other words, Chas had never been a 'pub' man which was one of John's habits). I know what that meant: Chas didn't make a regular evening call to his 'local' as John did, entering to cries of 'Hello! Veale!' and offers of drinks all round with John the centre of attention with his jokes and rounds of beer. Charles was friendless, colourless, and had a boring life with a complete lack of seductive prowess when it came to achieving sexual satisfaction with every attractive woman he met.

This was the ideal moment for a slice of sound brotherly advice for me. "You," he said, "now you are alone, must guard against becoming even more boring than you were before."

During this emotionally highly unsupportive family get-together, Lally sat in complete silence. She was obviously not going to take any part in it and we sat down to lunch. I suppose there was small talk and chats about the weather.

I drove them to Paddington and returned to Holmead Road, tears streaming down my face feeling that our house had been violated, particularly Charles's favourite chair, which John had occupied for his lecture. Before braving 4 Holmead Road, I did something very uncharacteristic. I called in on Nell Dunn, and wept copiously. She understood how deeply, terribly hurt I had been and her support gave me enough strength to do two things, I telephoned Lally to ask what she had thought about John's attack and whether she had mentioned it on the journey back to Oxford. She said she really hadn't been listening to John and there had been no discussion of the day between them. Again no sisterly interest in me and my sadness.

I then wrote to John telling him that after what he had said, I thought we shouldn't meet again for some time. I had his reply by return of post. He wrote that he was glad to get my letter as he had been trying for ages to think of a way of avoiding seeing me. After that, we only saw each other at family gatherings at which Robert and someone else acted as 'minders' for me so that we barely exchanged any words at all. The break lasted until he was dying, when I was persuaded that I might feel a sense of relief if I organised some kind of reconciliation. I arranged this with Robert's help, and John seemed pleased, but much more important for me was preserving a very affectionate relationship with John's daughter, Sarah and her family.

It seems strange that despite Charles' and my lack of friends and wit, and with both of us being so boring, that John and his on/off mistress were frequent weekend visitors in Beaconsfield and Holmead Road. They were always happy to be treated to drinks and meals, theatres and concerts and driving round London at night to see the lights and to have John pointing out to us the many houses where he had had sexual encounters with a variety of women whose responses were described in detail to Chas and me – and, of course, to the current mistress.

I felt suicidal after Charles died, and then, when Robert and I went to the cottage in France for a few days, quite suddenly one night as I was settling down to sleep I realised that I wasn't ready to die and that I must carry on living, however dreary it was.

Back in London, I began to take more interest in reading, music and seeing friends, and then a very odd thing happened.

Two old friends, John Nickson and Simon Rew, had been to supper with me and after they left I was in the kitchen clearing up when I had a nasty frightening feeling of déjà vu. I had had such feelings in Beaconsfield and had been prescribed pills but on moving in with Truman had stopped them with no return of symptoms.

Out of the blue, I was overwhelmed with exactly the same sense of panic. The next day, I went to my GP and asked for a prescription for the original drug. Instead, she referred me to a neurologist, Dr Angus Kennedy, who suggested tests, and after they were done he referred me to a psychotherapist, Dr Niall Campbell, with whom I felt instantly at ease. Dr Campbell, during my sessions with him, heard everything that is in this book as well as everything that I thought and felt during the times between sessions.

My first contact with him was by telephone, when he rang to arrange an appointment for me and I heard his warm voice and gentle Irish accent. Then, at our first session, I responded immediately to his looks. He is tall with thick, straight brown hair, not cut short. He has even, strong features and wide green eyes. Most noticeable was his relaxed personality and the way he bowed his head over his desk to laugh at my graphic and, I suppose, humorous descriptions of my family: Lally being as ugly as sin and as thick as two planks, for example. I also noted that he had the slightly round shoulders of a scholar. He was formally dressed in a dark suit, pastel shirt and patterned (not old school) tie.

We still meet at the Priory Hospital in Roehampton every two weeks, which means that for an hour every other week, I shall not be alone and can tell Dr Campbell everything I need to talk about, knowing that he will never let me down. I can telephone him between meetings if I need to discuss anything.

There is absolutely nothing he doesn't know and understand about me and everyone I know as well as my immediate family

Quite soon, Dr Campbell became the central figure in my life. The relationship between us, his as a professional and mine as a patient with a story needing to be told, and the problems resulting from it are of course unique. Our meetings allow me to express all my emotions, even, on occasions, anger with him, depressions, family problems and, important to me, my feelings of love for him and the resulting freedom I feel for others and affection for people in general.

All these are acceptable subjects for discussion. Often, though, we talk about books, TV programmes, films, politics – anything that springs to mind – and one of the best things for me is when he tells me about his family.

Soon after my first session with Dr Campbell was the good news from Camberwell that Robert had met another actor, Kate Duchêne, who had been in a play with Mick Ford, and she was moving in with Robert. Robert arranged for Kate and me to meet at a theatre. I told her later that I had been afraid that she might not like me. Kate also feared that she might not like me. It seems that our fears were groundless.

Around this time, I was standing at a bus stop on the New Kings Road, just having missed two buses. A tall American joined me at the stop and I remarked that I had seen two buses pass just before I arrived. He said, reassuringly, that there would be another one soon. He was wrong. There was a long wait during which he asked me how I was feeling on this lovely spring morning. I told him I was overjoyed, as I had just got my printer to work.

The bus was so delayed that we had a very long time to discuss films, books, music, operas and theatres. His name was Art Rubino and, as the bus finally arrived, he had time to ask me if he might email me and for me to give him my email address.

His smile and voice were charming; he was overweight, but I was so pleased at having someone to talk to that I barely noticed it. I did not see him get off the bus, so did my shopping and forgot about him.

A day or two after meeting Art, Robert and I went to the cottage in France for a few days, and when I came home there was an email from Art saying how much he had enjoyed meeting me and inviting me to go to a concert with him, with the tactful suggestion that we should meet at the concert venue. The concert had been while I was in Fillièvres, as I explained by email to Art, who then invited me out to dinner at a restaurant.

He called for me in his ancient Porsche and during the meal he told me that he and his wife lived separately, he working as a computer consultant in London, she staying in New Mexico, their two adult children, a son and daughter, near her. We discovered that when Chas and I were in Holland, Art had been working in The Hague, when Chas and I moved to Surrey, he had a flat near the Albert Hall, when we had moved to Beaconsfield he was living in Iver Heath and his children were at school in Beaconsfield. Lastly, when Chas and I moved to Holmead Road, Art was living very near in Wandsworth Bridge Road.

This was not the end of the coincidences. Art's birthday was February 26th, the day before mine, his son David's birthday was March 6th, the day before Robert's and his daughter Diana's birthday was on July 4th, the day before that of Robert's partner, Kate. It seemed to me that fate had had a hand in our meeting, though Robert, unromantically, maintained that it was all simply coincidental.

The start of my affair with Art came one evening. We had been out to dinner and came back to Holmead Road to listen to CDs. I was standing at the player with my back to him and he came over behind me and very gently enfolded me in his arms. I instinctively leant back against him. It felt like reaching a safe haven.

When I told all this to Dr Campbell he seemed to be impressed by Art's tactful and diplomatic courtship of me. I remember reclining on Art's sofa while he crossed the road for fish and chips for supper and thinking, I am happy, better still, I am content. I have Dr Campbell to whom I can turn whenever

I need him and I have an American lover who wants to be with me as often as I want him to be. Art sometimes had to go to the States for work, but whether he was there or here, we telephoned and emailed each other several times a day and even in the night.

I went to Wandsworth Bridge Road for the nights we spent together, although my studio was available when we felt like it. The snag with the studio was that so many stairs were not good for Art's health, as he had had a heart bypass as well as being diabetic. When we first went out together, I had told him I hated cooking and would not be returning his hospitality, to which he answered, "I want to cook for you and I enjoy cooking so that's alright." We were always content to stay in and we played Scrabble, watched TV and he taught me to play Gin Rummy.

I usually won Scrabble and he almost always won Gin Rummy, as he had been a very good Bridge player.

Best of all, he was a tender, exciting, inventive lover so, having both been deprived of physical relationships for so long, this made for the most full and satisfying relationship.

There were, of course, disagreements and I had to persuade him that arguing was not the same as quarrelling. Art was a Republican and I found arguing with him, with my very left wing views, stimulating. I gathered he told his wife and family what to think politically. I persuaded him that capital punishment was not acceptable under any circumstances and that America and Britain could not impose democracy on another country, such as Iraq. These arguments were lengthy, friendly and had to be logical. And I was not prepared to be told what to think by anyone.

With Art always wanting me, and with Dr Campbell to help me over the problems that arose from Art having to abandon pills and inject himself for his worsening diabetes, we were very happy together, except that I fretted about Kate and Robert, who were desperate to start a family. IVF seemed their only hope. It was a roller coaster of emotions for them, enduring brilliant but increasingly cautious flashes of hope, as hopes were crushed by the despair of miscarriages.

At a particularly low period, Art's health worsened, and I would wake up in an empty bed to find him, lost in thought, sitting in his living-room. He would only tell me that he hadn't been able to sleep, but I know now that he was contemplating returning to America to die. The sale of his flat followed with lame explanations to me about work to do in the States, but promises of frequent future visits to London, interspersed with declarations of how truly he always had and always would love me.

He told me that Diana and David were coming to Fulham to fly back to New Mexico with him. His family had never heard of me and we had to secretly exchange our house keys to each other's houses. I knew I must not appear when his family came, yet he seemed unconcerned about a possible meeting.

Maybe he thought he might explain the apparently inexplicable situation to them – that he hadn't managed to live year after year in London without any female companionship of any kind.

I have an email folder of messages between us, some of them acrimonious on my part. Before one of his visits to America I had said how worried I would be if a day or two passed without news of him and so he gave me David's telephone number to ring if this happened.

He left Fulham and after four days I was so worried I telephoned David. He wanted to know who I was and how I knew his father. I hedged, saying Art had helped me with my computer. How well had I known his father, David persisted. Again I hedged, but then David asked me if I wore a red coat, to which I owned up. David, clearly upset, told me he had found a photograph of me in his father's wallet. It transpired that on reaching home, Art had collapsed in the entrance to his house and died.

The funeral had been arranged and neither he nor his mother or sister wanted ever to have anything to do with me. I interrupted long enough during the call to say how much Art cared about them all, especially Diana's children, his grandchildren. As we spoke, I was truly sorry for them all but Art and I had made each other less lonely and much happier and that is something I shall never regret.

Art had met my family and friends and they all very much approved of our affair. I had also introduced him to my GP, Dr Sandberg, and my dentist, David Kaplan and they were most sympathetic towards me but, most of all, Robert and Kate were sorry to see me forlorn and helped me bear another loss. Dr Campbell, as ever, fulfilled his role as my lifeline. Never having to put on a brave face, not to have to "rise to the occasion" or act in a socially acceptable manner, but to be encouraged to reveal feelings and cry if the need arises, is the experience I have with Dr Campbell. It is psychotherapy at its most healing, a treatment which is completely objective on the part of the psychiatrist whose responses are clever, presenting new ideas and choices and suggesting with warmth and care, possible solutions to problems.

I remember at the end of one session, when I had only seen him a few times and had had a very grim time, Dr Campbell shook hands as usual but put his other hand over mine and said, "We do care, you know."

The void left by Art, though not exactly filled, was soothed later in the summer by the news that at last IVF had worked for Kate, and she was pregnant. Friends and relatives assure mothers-to-be that morning sickness wears off, but in our case, every morning when I rang them, I asked if Kate was feeling a bit sick and if she was, we were jubilant. On April 15th, Anna was born in a birth pool in Coleman Road, Camberwell and there should be a blue plaque on the wall of that house now to celebrate her arrival. Not only had she been longed for, she was also a pretty baby and alert and intelligent from the very beginning.

She makes a noticeable impact on people wherever she goes. From her earliest days her shining blue eyes would focus on adults speaking to each other as though she understood every word they said. Robert took her into the National Theatre where Kate was to act very soon after the birth to be fed by Kate during rehearsals. Anna learnt to hold court, regally extending her hand to be kissed by admiring dressers, actors, directors and friends.

Later, this dialogue occurred between Kate and Anna:–

Kate: Anna, please pass me that pen.

Anna: No.

Kate: Why won't you pass it to me?

Anna: I can't

Kate: Why can't you?

Anna: Because I don't want to.

When Anna was three, another IVF treatment was successful and not only was Kate pregnant again, but with eggs from the same donor who had donated Anna's, making them true siblings and a complete family.

Charlie's birth was announced by Robert telephoning to tell me that he knew I would find Charlie acceptable as he had a lot of brown hair and large blue eyes.

Lying on his back, a few months old, he looks into my eyes, and round the room when I bend over him and speak and smile, and then he smiles and laughs a long, gurgling laugh.

୶୶

So, after a grim and gruesome start in life, and a feeling I always had that life itself was a darkly dubious blessing, I observe the precise opposite in Robert, Kate, Anna and Charlie. They all find life interesting, fulfilling, rewarding and, reassuringly to me, fun... As far as they are concerned, I have made my contribution to lives worth living.

※

I was the victim of a mother suffering from Munchausen's syndrome by proxy and a father with psychopathic tendencies. On balance, I think the wounds they inflicted have been more than offset by the discovery of a world in which there are understanding and supportive friends such as Rudi and the long, slow and sometimes painful process of facing hidden truths with the help and guidance of psychotherapists. Robert and his family are the major protagonists in the wonderful world that has such people in it.

www.ingramcontent.com/pod-product-compliance
Lightning Source LLC
Chambersburg PA
CBHW022101160426
43198CB00008B/306